CliffsN

Anthem

By Andrew Bernstein, Ph.D.

IN THIS BOOK

- Learn about the life, background, and philosophy of Ayn Rand
- Preview an introduction to *Anthem*
- Explore the novel's themes and character development in the Critical Commentaries
- Examine in-depth Character Analyses
- Acquire an understanding of the novel with Critical Essays
- Reinforce what you learn with CliffsNotes Review
- Find additional information to further your study in CliffsNotes Resource Center and online at www.cliffsnotes.com

WILEY

Wiley Publishing, Inc.

About the Author

Andrew Bernstein holds a Ph.D.in Philosophy from the Graduate School of the City University of New York. He teaches Philosophy at Pace University in Pleasantville, New York, and at the State University of New York at Purchase. Dr. Bernstein is a speaker for the Ayn Rand Institute and lectures on Ayn Rand's novels throughout the United States.

Publisher's Acknowledgments
Editorial

Project Editor: Michael Kelly
Acquisitions Editor: Gregory W. Tubach
Editorial Administrator: Michelle Hacker
Glossary Editors: The editors and staff of Webster's New World Dictionaries
Production
Indexer: York Production Services, Inc.
Proofreader: York Production Services, Inc.
Wiley Indianapolis Composition Services

CliffsNotes™ *Anthem*

Published by:
Wiley Publishing, Inc.
111 River Street
Hoboken, NJ 07030
www.wiley.com

Copyright © 2000 Wiley Publishing, Inc., Hoboken, NJ

10 9 8 7 6 5 4 3 2
1O/RT/RT/QT/IN
Published by Wiley Publishing, Inc., Hoboken, NJ
Published simultaneously in Canada

Library of Congress Cataloging-in-Publication Data
Berstein, Andrew.
    CliffsNotes Rand's Anthem by Andrew Bernstein.
        p.   cm.
    Includes bibliographical references and index.
    ISBN 0-7645-8557-6 (alk. paper)
    1.Rand, Ayn. Anthem -- examinations -- Study guides. 2. Individuality in literature. 3. Time travel in literature. I. Title: Anthem. II. Title.
PS3535.A547 A733 2000
813'.52--dc21   00–039526
                                                      CIP

For general information on our other products and services or to obtain technical support, please contact our Customer Care Department within the U.S. at 800-762-2974, outside the U.S. at 317-572-3993, or fax 317-572-4002.

Wiley also publishes its books in a variety of electronic formats. Some content that appears in print may not be available in electronic books.

Table of Contents

How to Use This Book

This CliffsNotes study guide on Ayn Rand's *Anthem* supplements the original literary work, giving you background information about the author, an introduction to the work, a graphical character map, critical commentaries, expanded glossaries, and a comprehensive index, all for you to use as an educational tool that will allow you to better understand *Anthem*. This study guide was written with the assumption that you have read *Anthem*. Reading a literary work doesn't mean that you immediately grasp the major themes and devices used by the author; this study guide will help supplement your reading to be sure you get all you can from Ayn Rand's *Anthem*. CliffsNotes Review tests your comprehension of the original text and reinforces learning with questions and answers, practice projects, and more. For further information on Ayn Rand and *Anthem,* check out the CliffsNotes Resource Center.

CliffsNotes provides the following icons to highlight essential elements of particular interest:

Reveals the underlying themes in the work.

Helps you to more easily relate to or discover the depth of a character.

Uncovers elements such as setting, atmosphere, mystery, passion, violence, irony, symbolism, tragedy, foreshadowing, and satire.

Enables you to appreciate the nuances of words and phrases.

Don't Miss Our Web Site

Discover classic literature as well as modern-day treasures by visiting the CliffsNotes Web site at www.cliffsnotes.com. You can obtain a quick download of a CliffsNotes title, purchase a title in print form, browse our catalog, or view online samples.

LIFE AND BACKGROUND OF THE AUTHOR

The following abbreviated biography of Rand is provided so that you might become more familiar with her life and the historical times that possibly influenced her writing. Read this Life and Background of the Author section and recall it when reading Ayn Rand's *Anthem*, thinking of any thematic relationship between Rand's novel and her life.

Personal Background

Ayn Rand was born Alissa Rosenbaum in 1905 in St. Petersburg, Russia. Rand was raised in an upper-middle-class, European-oriented family, in the midst of the mysticism and nationalism of Russia. Having taught herself to read, Rand, at the age of 8, became captivated by the heroism in a French-language serial adventure titled *The Mysterious Valley*. At the age of 9, Rand decided to become a writer, inspired especially by Victor Hugo's novels. Hugo's writing helped arm her against the fatalistic view of life that dominated Russia, a country she later described as "an accidental cesspool of civilization."

Education and Early Life

In February of 1917, Ayn Rand witnessed the first shots of the Russian Revolution, and later that year she witnessed the Bolshevik Revolution as well. In order to escape the fighting, her family went to the Crimea, where Rand finished high school. The final Communist victory brought the confiscation of her father's pharmacy and periods of near-starvation. When introduced to American history in her last year of high school, Rand immediately took America as her model of what a nation of free men could be. Her love for the West—especially America—was fueled by the Viennese operettas and American and German films, which the Soviets temporarily allowed to be shown.

When Rand and her family returned from the Crimea, she entered the University of Petrograd to study philosophy and history, graduating in 1924. She entered the State Institute for Cinema Arts in 1924 to study screenwriting. During this period, Rand produced her first formal writings, essays about Hollywood, published in 1999 by The Ayn Rand Institute Press as *Russian Writings on Hollywood*.

Immigration to the United States

In late 1925, Ayn Rand obtained permission to leave the Soviet Union to visit relatives in the United States, on the pretext of learning the American film business. After six months with relatives in Chicago, she moved to Hollywood to pursue a career as a screenwriter. On her second day there, she had a chance meeting with her favorite American director, Cecil B. DeMille, who took her to the set of his epic film *The King of Kings* and gave her a job, first as an extra, then as a script reader.

During the next week at the studio, she met an actor, Frank O'Connor, whom she married in 1929; they were married until his death 50 years later.

Career Highlights

After struggling for several years at various non-writing jobs, including one in the wardrobe department at the RKO film studio, Rand sold her first screenplay, *Red Pawn*, to Universal Studios in 1932. Rand saw her first stage play, *Night of January 16th*, produced in Hollywood in 1934 and then on Broadway in 1935. Her first novel, *We the Living*, was completed in 1933. The most autobiographical of Rand's novels, *We the Living* was rejected as too anti-Communist and wasn't published in the United States until 1936. In 1937, Rand devoted a few weeks to write her novella *Anthem*, which was soon published in England but was not published in the United States until 1947, ten years later.

Although positively reviewed, neither *We the Living* nor *Anthem* garnered high sales. Not until the publication of *The Fountainhead* did Ayn Rand achieve fame. Rand began writing *The Fountainhead* in 1935, taking seven years to complete the book. In the hero of *The Fountainhead*, architect Howard Roark, she presented for the first time the kind of hero whose depiction was the chief goal of her writing: the ideal man, man "as he could be and ought to be." *The Fountainhead* was rejected by 12 publishers but finally accepted by Bobbs-Merrill. Although published in 1943, *The Fountainhead* made history by becoming a bestseller two years later, through word-of-mouth, and it gained for its author lasting recognition as a champion of individualism.

Ayn Rand returned to Hollywood in late 1943 to write the screenplay for *The Fountainhead*, but wartime restrictions delayed production until 1948. Working part-time as a screenwriter for producer Hal Wallis, Rand wrote such scripts as *Love Letters* and *You Came Along*, and she began her major novel, *Atlas Shrugged*, in 1946. In 1951, Rand permanently moved back to New York City and devoted herself full-time to the completion of the novel *Atlas Shrugged*. Despite extremely negative reviews, *Atlas Shrugged* quickly became a bestseller.

Rand's Philosophy: Objectivism

After the publication of *Atlas Shrugged* in 1957, Ayn Rand realized that she would have to identify the philosophy that made her heroes possible. She termed this philosophy Objectivism and described it as "a philosophy for living on earth." Rand offered private courses on both fiction and nonfiction writing and, in 1958, helped form an institute to teach her philosophy. For the remaining years of her life, Rand devoted herself to nonfiction writing, penning and editing a number of articles for her periodicals. These articles later appeared in numerous philosophic collections and dealt with topics including ethics (*The Virtue of Selfishness*), politics (*Capitalism: the Unknown Ideal*), aesthetics (*The Romantic Manifesto*), and the theory of knowledge (*Introduction to Objectivist Epistemology*). At the time of her death in 1982, Rand was working on a television miniseries of *Atlas Shrugged*.

A controversial novelist and philosopher—especially in academic circles—Ayn Rand attained widespread recognition, as indicated by a 1991 joint survey by The Library of Congress and The Book-of-the-Month Club, which placed *Atlas Shrugged* as second only to the Bible as the most influential book among American readers. The Ayn Rand Society (a subgroup of the American Philosophical Association), an Ayn Rand first-class postage stamp (issued by The U.S. Postal Service in 1999), and an Academy Award-nominated documentary about her life (*Ayn Rand: A Sense of Life*, 1997) also serve as proof of her influence. The Ayn Rand Institute in Marina del Rey, California, was established in 1985 to increase the awareness of the existence and content of Ayn Rand's philosophy.

INTRODUCTION TO THE NOVEL

The following Introduction section is provided solely as an educational tool and is not meant to replace the experience of your reading the novel. Read the Introduction and A Brief Synopsis to enhance your understanding of the novel and to prepare yourself for the critical thinking that should take place whenever you read any work of fiction or nonfiction. Keep the List of Characters and Character Map at hand so that as you read the original literary work, if you encounter a character about whom you're uncertain, you can refer to the List of Characters and Character Map to refresh your memory.

Introduction

Anthem is an outstanding introduction to Ayn Rand's philosophy of human nature. The novella's theme and central conflict—the individual versus the collective—occurs in all her novels and is an important element of her moral and political philosophy.

The story of *Anthem* takes place in an unnamed Communist- or Fascist-like dictatorship of the future, where an individual has no rights, existing solely to serve the state. The hero, Equality 7-2521, is a brilliant young man who yearns to be a scientist, but who is commanded to be a Street Sweeper by a government that fears his independence of mind.

The citizens of this society are pawns without rights who exist as wards of the state. They are born in state-controlled hospitals, raised in state-controlled nurseries, educated in state-controlled schools, toil at state-assigned jobs, and sleep in massive barracks organized by the state. Citizens have no personal lives or loves; they cannot choose friends or lovers. Instead, they engage in state-controlled breeding, in which the government decides who sleeps with whom and when. Even their names are variations on collectivist slogans—Unity, Fraternity, International, and so on—followed by numbers, indicating the many "brothers" who share the slogan for a name. Above all, the word "I" has been outlawed; it is the "Unspeakable Word" that has been erased from the language and from the thoughts of citizens. All first-person references have been expunged from individual thought. When individuals speak of themselves, they use the collective "we," there being no individualistic concepts or words available.

The struggle of Equality 7-2521 to think, live, and love on his own terms and in conflict with the oppressive dictatorship forms the heart of *Anthem*. By means of her character's quest, Ayn Rand defends the right of individuals to a life of their own and sounds a warning against modern society's relentless movement toward collectivism. The novella is informed with a sense of urgency derived from the popularity of various collectivist factions existing at the time of its writing (that continue to exist to this day.) In the 1930s, a number of U.S. intellectuals and politicians praised both the Nazi and Communist systems as "noble experiments"—and support for Communism, as Marxist ideology, continues among many American intellectuals.

Ayn Rand was born in Russia in 1905 and raised during the Russian Revolution. She saw firsthand the horrors of Communism in action. She witnessed the confiscation of private property, the persecution (and disappearance) of political dissidents, and through reports from her family that remained in Russia, the extermination of millions by Josef Stalin. Escaping to America—the freest country in history—she was horrified to find present and increasingly popular the very ideas she had fled. Leading up to World War II, American intellectuals and politicians often lauded the Fascist, Nazi, and Communist regimes in Italy, Germany, and Russia as "noble experiments."

Many American leaders admired the Fascists and Communists for their undeviating commitment to the belief that an individual exists solely to serve society. President Franklin Delano Roosevelt, though certainly not an advocate of totalitarianism, implemented, in the New Deal, a myriad of programs that were loosely based on the premise that moral virtue resides exclusively in selfless service to others. Before the war, moral support existed in the United States for both the Communists and the Nazis; even after the war, support for Communism persisted among the intellectuals, as it does to this day. Ayn Rand wrote *Anthem* in the 1930s as a warning to Western civilization about the horrors of collectivism, whether of the Nazi or Communist variety.

Without doubt, the most strikingly original feature of the book is its use of language. In the society depicted in the story, the process of collectivization has been completed at a level far deeper than the political. This society has successfully brainwashed its citizens to believe that only toil for others is good, and that they should exist utterly bereft of a personal life. The collectivist masters have also succeeded in radically altering the thought patterns of its citizens. Leaders have obliterated all concepts of individuality from human minds. Concepts such as "I," "me," or any other individualistic, first-person references have been extirpated from language and from human thinking. Only collectivist thought and speech are permitted. Individuals think and speak of themselves only as "we."

The state has succeeded in collectivizing society not only in political practice but also at the deepest level of thought. The situation is reminiscent of Hitler's claim that National Socialism was more effectively collectivist than Communism because, as he put it, "The Communists nationalize banks and industries, whereas we [the Nazis] nationalize bankers and industrialists," that is, humans.

Another memorable aspect of this story is the depiction of a collectivist society as regressing into scientific, technological, and industrial collapse. In *Anthem*, Ayn Rand portrays a Dark Age of the future. Her vision of a collectivized society stands in sharp contrast to that of George Orwell as presented in his novel, *1984*. Orwell and Rand agree about the moral horrors of such a society—the utter lack of individual rights, the slave labor, the indoctrination, the inability to think or speak freely, the terror, and the oppressive sense of futility under these conditions. But Orwell projects a totalitarian state of scientific and technological advance. In *1984*, spectacular progress in the hard sciences has created the ability to engage in thought control. *Anthem*, on the other hand, shows that a prohibition of freedom results in a decline into primitive subsistence. What is the fundamental philosophical conviction that leads Rand to the belief that a collectivist society is doomed to Dark Age backwardness? Her theory that progress and scientific knowledge are products of independent minds.

Observe the unflagging curiosity of Equality 7-2521's intellect. Though forbidden, he dissects animals, melts metals, mixes acids, and raises a lightning rod. He explores and experiments, until finally, he discovers the "power of the sky." Although he explicitly accepts the social judgment that to think and act alone is evil—and though he realizes that, if caught, he will be executed—his desire to understand the laws of nature supersedes all of this. "[It] was our curse," he says, "which drove us to our crime. We had been a good Street Sweeper and like all our brother Street Sweepers, save for our cursed wish to know. We looked too long at the stars at night, and at the trees and the earth." Despite everything a hostile society might do to him, Equality 7-2521 is driven by one all-consuming passion: He must know. He possesses the soul, as well as the intellect, of a great scientist.

By virtue of this kind of unshakeable independence, Rand argues, humankind forges ahead, moving from ignorance to enlightenment. Many of society's great thinkers and innovators were persecuted in much the same way that Equality 7-2521 is. For example, Socrates was executed for the originality of his moral principles. Galileo was threatened with torture by the Inquisition for daring to defend Copernicus, and his contemporary, Giordano Bruno, was burned at the stake. Charles Darwin was damned for originating, and John Scopes jailed for teaching, the theory of evolution. Robert Fulton was scorned, Henry Ford mocked, and Louis Pasteur reviled because of their inventions or new ideas.

The court of social opinion has generally convicted freethinkers. But by being freethinkers, the Equality 7-2521s of the world are unconcerned about the evaluations of others. Free thought and action continue. But when an innovator like Equality 7-2521 is caught in a political dictatorship that physically prevents him from researching, experimenting, or studying, then the creative mind is stifled.

But the mind must be left free to think and to act on its findings, which is the deepest principle lying at the heart of this story. In a free society, an original thinker like Equality 7-2521 is free to experiment and research, to invent and innovate, and to make scientific breakthroughs and technological advances. This concept is why the world's freest countries have made so many discoveries and have achieved such a high standard of living. Science and progress require intellectual freedom. A totalitarian state stifles the freedom of mind that such progress depends on. A worldwide totalitarian state, as depicted in *Anthem*, leaves the mind with no refuge. Thinkers like Equality 7-2521 have no place to go. They are trapped in a system that stifles freethinking. Rand argues that a society in which the mind is stifled will not merely fail to progress, it will regress, losing all the advances that freer men have achieved, just as accomplishments of ancient Greek society were lost in the Dark Ages.

In defending the freedom of the mind as a necessity of human survival and prosperity, *Anthem* is a precursor to Ayn Rand's major novels, *The Fountainhead* and *Atlas Shrugged*. All of these works feature some aspect of this theme. *Anthem* shows the collapse into Dark-Age barbarism that results when the mind is stifled. *The Fountainhead* shows that the independent minds responsible for progress and prosperity are generally opposed by their societies, those most likely to benefit from innovation. *Atlas Shrugged* shows that the rational mind is humankind's survival instrument, as well as what happens to the world when its best thinkers go on strike. All of her subsequent fiction presents heroes such as Equality 7-2521, persons of unswerving loyalty to their independent judgment.

One final point is necessary to help us understand *Anthem*: The characters depicted—both those who think and those who unquestioningly obey—have free will, that is, they make choices. This free will is clearest in the heroic characters. Equality 7-2521 has a choice to go into the ancient subway tunnel or not, to report it or not, to steal away and study science or not, to flee into the Uncharted Forest or accept his fate, and so on. International 4-8818 similarly has a choice to report Equality 7-2521's actions or stand by his friend. The Golden One

(Liberty 5-3000) has the choice to follow her heart or the dictates of society, which prohibit her from speaking to Equality 7-2521. The Saint of the Pyre chooses not to repent his "crime" of uttering the Unspeakable Word, but instead picks out of the crowd the young Equality 7-2521 as his heir.

Further, the more passive characters also make choices; mindless obedience is not forced on them. The Council of Scholars, for example, must choose when Equality 7-2521 places before them the newly rediscovered electric light and pleads for its ability to rid human habitations of darkness. Much earlier, the Council of Vocations choose a profession for the clear-eyed young man who stands before it, and the members choose Street Sweeper. Finally, Equality 7-2521's fellow citizens—unlike him—do not choose to challenge the propaganda meted out by society, but simply accept passively. This choice is not forced on them. The citizens are not lashed into submission with whips. They are not brainwashed by means of drugs, deprivation, and torture. The streets do not crawl with secret police to report on those who question the state. Rather, the citizens voluntarily obey, because to do so is much easier than to face the wracking questions that a thinker like Equality 7-2521 confronts.

Students often think that the citizens of *Anthem* are mindless puppets, brainwashed and controlled by the state. This is not so. The citizens retain their capacity to think and to choose. Equality 7-2521's plan, at the end, depends on this free will—for when he creates a different kind of society, he fully expects the best among humankind to recognize the society's merit and flock to its banner. They will choose freedom over tyranny. The mind may lie dormant, but never extinct; no dictatorship can kill the human capacity to choose liberty.

A Brief Synopsis

The story of *Anthem* takes place in some unspecified future time and place in which freedom and individual rights have been obliterated. Collectivism—the political philosophy holding that an individual exists solely to serve the state—is dominant and has led to the establishment of a global dictatorship of the Fascist or Communist variety.

Equality 7-2521 is a Street Sweeper of the city, having been chosen for this profession by the Council of Vocations. However, he has always been fascinated by the phenomena of nature and can't help but wonder what power of the sky causes lightning and how it can be harnessed to human benefit. Because of his fascination with the Science of Things, he secretly desires to be sent to the Home of the Scholars. He has been taught that it is a sin to harbor secret ambitions, and so believes he is guilty, though strangely, he feels no pangs of wrongdoing.

One day while sweeping the streets, Equality 7-2521 comes upon a metal grill leading down into a dark tunnel. The tunnel is clearly a remnant of the Unmentionable Times, the ancient period prior to the establishment of the present society. Equality 7-2521 sneaks to the tunnel alone every night, where safe from others beneath the ground he secretly performs scientific experiments. As the story opens, this private research has been occurring for two years.

In that time, he also meets Liberty 5-3000. She is a young woman who works in the fields and lives in the Home of the Peasants beyond the city. Men and women are forbidden to take notice of each other except at the Time of Mating, the period each spring when the Council of Eugenics pairs off men and women into couples for one night for the purpose of procreating. But in his own mind, Equality 7-2521 takes such notice of Liberty 5-3000 that he gives her a different name. He thinks of her as the Golden One. He commits yet another transgression by speaking to her, and it is clear that she takes notice of him.

He has forbidden thoughts. In the night, he wonders about the Uncharted Forests that exist across the land, covering the cities of the Unmentionable Times. He thinks of the Script Fire in which the books of the Evil Ones were burned, and he wonders about the secrets of the Evil Ones that have been lost to the world. Mostly, he wonders about the Unspeakable Word, the one idea held by the Evil Ones that has been lost. He remembers the fate of one who had discovered that word and had spoken it. His tongue had been ripped out, and he was burned at the stake. As a 10-year-old child, Equality 7-2521 had witnessed the execution. The transgressor seemed noble, and the child had thought that this was the face of one of the Saints about whom children had been taught. To the young Equality 7-2521, this Saint of the Pyre seemed to have gazed at him, picking him out from the crowd of onlookers. What, he wonders late at night, is the Unspeakable Word?

In his experiments, Equality 7-2521 discovers electricity. He uses it, after much effort, to create an electric light. He thinks that this light can be used to light the cities of the world. He wishes to show it to others, but knows that they will not understand and be frightened. In a month, the World Council of Scholars meets in his city. He knows what to do. The wisest minds among humankind will be there. They are the only ones who can understand his gift. He will wait and show it to them, and they will know how best to employ it for the good of society. And he will be welcomed among them as one of the Scholars.

But when he demonstrates his invention, they are frightened. They call him an "evil wretch" for daring to think that a lowly Street Sweeper can possess greater wisdom than that of the Council. He has broken all the laws, and must be severely punished. Equality 7-2521 acknowledges that they are right and does not care what happens to him. But the light, he pleads. What will you do with the light? They point out that he is alone in believing that he has invented a great new product—and that what is not believed by all cannot be true. They point out that if he is right, then his discovery will bring ruin to the Department of Candles and confusion to the Plans of the World Council. For it took 50 years to get approval for the candle from all the Councils, and to change the Plans again so soon would be impossible. Their conclusion is unanimous: The light is an evil thing and must be destroyed.

Before they can seize it, he takes it in his arms, smashes the glass of the window with his fist and leaps through it. He runs through the streets of the city, escaping to the Uncharted Forest. He doesn't know where he is going—indeed there is no place to go—but he must get away. He believes that he will perish in the forest. He accepts that and is not afraid, only he wishes to be away from the city and from "air that touches upon the air of the city." He plunges deeper into the Uncharted Forest.

But he does not die. He awakens on the first day in the forest with a realization of freedom. There is no longer anyone to tell him what to do. The next day, he hears footsteps behind him. He hides in the bushes, but there is no need, for it is the Golden One. She had heard of his escape, because the whole city is speaking of it. On the night that she heard it, she bolted from the Home of the Peasants and followed his trail through the forest. She says she would rather be damned with him than blessed with all her brothers. He takes her in his arms, and that night he discovers that to make love to a woman is "the one ecstasy granted to the race of men." He is frightened only by the realization that he had lived for 21 years and never known what joy is possible to men.

They come upon an abandoned home from the Unmentionable Times. They enter it and wonder at the sights they behold—at the bright colors, the mirrors, the clothes, and the books. Equality 7-2521 declares that the home will be theirs. He finds that the books are written in the language that he speaks, and he reads them.

In his reading, he discovers the word "I." When he grasps its meaning, he cries tears of deliverance, realizing that this is the holy word that humans have had taken away from them. His reading teaches him that persons are individuals, not splintered fragments of the group; they have a right to pursue their happiness, and should not sacrifice themselves for others; that they require freedom to do this, and must not be enslaved by the group. When he understands this, he takes for himself a name he finds in his reading—Prometheus—the bringer of fire. The Golden One takes the name of Gaea—the goddess who was the mother of the earth. Gaea is pregnant with his child, who will be the first-born of a new society of free humans.

Equality 7-2521 learns that his light is powered by electricity, and that the men of the Unmentionable Times had mastered it. He will learn what they knew and use the knowledge to create prosperity. He will build electric wires around his house to protect it and will steal back into the city to free his friend, International 4-8818, and any others who flock to the banner of liberty. The society he founds will make scientific and technological advances because the human mind will not be shackled; it will be free to think, to ask questions, and to explore. He believes that, in time, the world will hear of this free and prosperous society, and that the best individuals from around the globe will flood the roads leading to his city. They will live together in respect of each individual's right to live his or her own life.

List of Characters

Equality 7-2521 (Prometheus) The hero of the story. He is a man of unbending independence living in a dark age of a future totalitarian state. The state commands him to be a Street Sweeper, but he is fascinated by science and secretly performs research on his own. He discovers the electric light, and ultimately hopes to lead the establishment of a freer society.

Liberty 5-3000 (Gaea) The young woman whom Equality 7-2521 loves. She is as spiritually unconquered as is the hero, and when he is damned by society, she follows him alone into the Uncharted Forest. She would rather die with the man of her choice than live in a society where individuality is prohibited.

International 4-8818 Friend of Equality 7-2521. Because there is laughter in his eyes—and because, with charcoal, he drew humorous pictures on walls—he was sent by the Council of Vocations to the Home of the Street Sweepers.

Saint of the Pyre A young man whom Equality 7-2521, in his youth, witnessed being burned at the stake. The man had discovered the Unspeakable Word. He seems to pick Equality 7-2521 from the crowd, seeking to communicate some meaning, an action that foreshadows Equality 7-2521's future.

Fraternity 2-5503 A Street Sweeper. He is "a quiet boy with wise, kind eyes, who cry suddenly, without reason." His body shakes with sobs that he cannot explain.

Solidarity 9-6347 Another Street Sweeper. He is bright and exhibits no fear in the day, but he screams in his sleep: "Help us! Help us!" in a voice that chills those who hear it. The doctors cannot cure him.

Evil Ones The leaders of an earlier capitalist era, prior to the current collectivist dictatorship. They believed that individuals had the right to their own lives and seek their own happiness and had established a system of political and economic freedom.

Collective 0-0009 The oldest and "wisest" of the World Council of Scholars. He condemns Equality 7-2521 for daring to think for himself. In his power lust and condemnation of independent thought, he represents all the governing Councils. Collective means group and is used in this culture to denote the utter submersion of an individual into the social whole.

Union 5-3992 Another Street Sweeper. He is "a sickly lad," who suffers from possessing "half a brain." The unfortunate Union 5-3992, in his ailment, is a symbol of collectivism: Collectivism prefers unthinking obedience to the independent mind.

Character Map

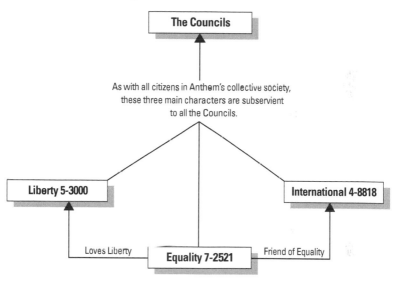

The Councils

As with all citizens in Anthem's collective society, these three main characters are subservient to all the Councils.

Liberty 5-3000

International 4-8818

Loves Liberty

Equality 7-2521

Friend of Equality

CRITICAL COMMENTARIES

The sections that follow provide great tools for supplementing your reading of *Anthem*. First, in order to enhance your understanding of and enjoyment from reading, we provide quick summaries in case you have difficulty when you read the original literary work. Each summary is followed by commentary: literary devices, character analyses, themes, and so on. Keep in mind that the interpretations here are solely those of the author of this study guide and are used to jumpstart your thinking about the work. No single interpretation of a complex work like *Anthem* is infallible or exhaustive, and you'll likely find that you interpret portions of the work differently from the author of this study guide. Read the original work and determine your own interpretations, referring to these Notes for supplemental meanings only.

Chapter 1

Summary

As the story opens, Equality 7-2521 states that it is a sin to do the writing he is doing. It is a sin to do things that do not involve others, and the words he thinks and writes are for no eyes or ears but his. This is not his only crime. He has committed one far worse and does not know what his punishment will be if discovered.

One day, as he sweeps the streets with International 4-8818, they find an iron grill buried beneath the weeds and papers blown from the nearby theatre. When they pull at it, the earth falls in and they find a series of steps leading into the darkness below. Equality 7-2521, though frightened, descends. He finds an abandoned tunnel, which he immediately realizes is a remnant of the Unmentionable Times, the ancient, evil period prior to the establishment of the current collectivist state. Though it is unthinkable, Equality 7-2521 tells International 4-8818 that they will not report the tunnel to the Council; rather, it belongs to him.

Each night after that, when his brothers sit in the darkened theatre watching plays about the virtue of toil, Equality 7-2521 steals away to his secret tunnel. There, hidden beneath the ground, he has three hours in which he does scientific research and performs experiments. He also steals manuscripts from the Scholars, and every night he studies. This activity goes on for two years.

Commentary

Theme

Equality 7-2521 is a freethinker living in a slave state. The state requires blind obedience to its decrees, which he refuses to render. He will not sacrifice his mind to the state's commands, the essence of the story's conflict. In *Anthem*, Ayn Rand shows the full reality of the ideals held by the Communists, Fascists, and their intellectual supporters. The underlying principle is *collectivism*: Society is paramount, and the individual must be subordinated to its dictates. Collectivists hold that an individual exists solely to serve the state and has no "inalienable right" to a free life or to the pursuit of happiness. Thus the citizens of this story are like mindless robots. They are not permitted to think for themselves; they must blindly obey the commands of the Councils.

In his conscious thinking, Equality 7-2521 accepts collectivism, because it is all he has been taught; nobody in this society has ever heard any different ideas. But implicitly, at the subconscious level, he holds and lives by the opposite premise, *individualism*: the theory that individuals have the right to think for themselves, to use their own minds and judgment in the pursuit of truth. Further, Equality 7-2521 believes that individuals have the right to *choose* what they want out of life—in this case, he has the right to pursue a career as a scientist because it is what he loves. Individuals, as Thomas Jefferson wrote in the *Declaration of Independence*, have an "inalienable right to life, liberty and the pursuit of happiness." In his individualism, Equality 7-2521 espouses the same ideals that form the heart of the American political system. In his rejection of collectivism, he shuns the principles of the Nazis and Communists.

The collectivism of this society explains why Equality 7-2521 is not permitted to think. If the individual must serve an all-powerful state, then it requires *obedience* from him. Collectivism values a blind, unquestioning allegiance—a willingness to follow orders unthinkingly. The Councils are in no danger from the mindless brutes of a society, whose strong backs are harnessed for manual labor. The Councils must fear only one foe: the freethinking mind. Equality 7-2521 represents a danger to them for he has the brainpower to question the moral rectitude of their regime—and the courage to stand by his convictions, even though his life is in danger.

Ayn Rand suggests that the reason dictators of all kinds—Fascist, Communist, or religious—always prohibit freedom of speech and of the press is that they are expressions of a deeper freedom of thought and encourage the free dissemination of ideas that collectivist societies dread. Dictators know that, in a free market of ideas, their arbitrary commands will be unable to withstand logical scrutiny. Therefore, they must ruthlessly suppress the right to think freely and to criticize their policies. Thus Equality 7-2521 is not allowed to think and is forbidden to study science.

Character Insight

Instead he is made a Street Sweeper. The teachers and Councils knew from his youth that his intelligence and eagerness to learn stood out. He was beyond his brothers and sisters in this respect. Because his questioning mind would not be stifled, he was punished continuously by the teachers—he was lashed more often than all the other children.

Two things were clear to the Councils: Equality 7-2521 had a mind of his own, and such a dangerous commodity was not to be encouraged. Therefore, he is consigned to the mindless task of sweeping the streets. Because he has the best mind, he is forbidden to think. Such is the inversion of collectivism, where things are the opposite of how they should be. Instead of glorifying the independent mind that invents the electric light and other advances—as they should—collectivist societies do everything in their power to stifle it.

The collectivist rulers understand that the essence of collectivism is conformity to the group. It is not just that individuals must serve the group in action. Deeper, they must accept and surrender their minds to its teachings. The foundation of Equality 7-2521's individualism is not pursuing his own happiness —this is a secondary consequence— but following his own mind. An individualist, such as Equality 7-2521, does not conform; he does not surrender the sovereign judgment of his own consciousness. He understands that to be a human being is to be a thinker. What makes someone an individual is a commitment to live by one's own best thinking—a refusal to betray one's mind, to yield the truth in order to follow the group. "To thine own self be true," says Polonius to Laertes in *Hamlet*. In *Anthem*, Ayn Rand shows that commitment to one's self is fundamentally commitment to one's mind.

A striking aspect of this society's war on the individual is its collectivization of the language, its eradication of all singular first-person references such as "I" or "me." By extirpating these words, the rulers have removed the possibility of even *thinking* in individualistic terms. From infancy, children are raised to think and speak of themselves only as "we." They are not permitted to know such a concept as "I." They know of an "Unspeakable Word," that to discover and speak that word is death, but they do not know what it is. In a brilliantly original indictment of collectivism, Ayn Rand points out that to fully subordinate the individual mind to society, collectivists must wipe out the very concept of an individual. If they succeed at this, there is no possibility of standing up to the stifling call for obedience; there is no independent mind to defend and no means by which to do so. The collectivists have wiped out individualism in language and in thought, as well as in action.

A further point raised in this chapter, which recurs throughout the story, is the struggle of an innovator against a society resistant to new ideas. Equality 7-2521 is like many of the great thinkers and scientists of history who have met hostility from the leaders of their times.

Socrates was put to death by Athenian society for the originality of his ideas. Galileo was threatened with torture by the Inquisition for defending the heliocentric theory in astronomy—and his earlier colleague, Giordano Bruno, was burned at the stake for the same reason. In free societies such as the United States, inventive thinkers such as Robert Fulton, the Wright brothers, and innovative architect Frank Lloyd Wright, merely face opposition from private citizens who follow tradition, but are not confronted with an all-powerful dictator who demands obedience. Such innovators are often mocked and ostracized, but not put to death. But Equality 7-2521 faces a collectivist state in which freethinking has been outlawed—much like an independent person in Nazi Germany or in Soviet Russia—and pursuit of new truths will result in his execution if apprehended. This risk is the fate of an innovator in a Fascist or Communist society. All who do not kneel and obey shall be imprisoned or executed.

Glossary

(Here and in the following chapters, difficult words and phrases, as well as allusions and historical references, are explained.)

World Council a global government that rules the entire world. In this world of the future, individuals possess no rights. The World Council is the highest governing body, the ultimate set of rulers who dictate policy to the rest of the world.

Unmentionable Times the days of the past when humans still possessed individual rights and political freedom. The dictators regard those past days as evil, because humans were living for themselves, not for others. It is unlawful to speak of these days when individuals were free to pursue their own happiness.

Great Truth the belief that human beings are not individuals but mere fragments of the whole. This society has been indoctrinated with the view that individuality is unreal, that the human race is like an ant colony in which each person is not a single, separate whole but an appendage of a larger social unity.

Great Rebirth the period in which the Unmentionable Times end and the one Great Truth is taught. During this time, political freedom is wiped out and belief in living for one's own happiness is eradicated. This is the beginning of the dictatorship in which humans must exist exclusively to serve their brothers and sisters.

Council of the Home the leaders of the particular barracks where a group of persons reside. Because this society supposedly has no individuals, all decisions are made by a sub-group that controls the larger group.

Council of Vocations the group of rulers whose specific function is to decide an individual's occupation. By forcing the best young minds into manual labor, the leaders hope to quell any potential intellectual dissent to their regime.

Home of the Scholars the residence of intellectuals and scientists whose task is to gain knowledge and discover new truths

Science of Things research into the phenomena of nature. This primitive society has only the most rudimentary of scientific knowledge, and it has regressed into a second Dark Age in which most knowledge of freer periods has been lost. This society believes the earth is flat, the sun revolves around it, and bleeding is a method of curing ailments.

The Transgression of Preference the "sin" of choice, which occurs when a person favors an activity or person based on independent judgment. Any exercise of independent evaluation is banned by this society.

Home of the Useless where the elderly of this society are sent at 40 years of age. They are thought to be too worn with toil to be of further use to society. This society is so lacking in knowledge of nutrition, medicine, and science that the life expectancy has shrunk back into the early 40s.

Chapter 2

Summary

Sweeping the streets on the edge of town, Equality 7-2521 notices a young woman toiling in the fields. Even though it is forbidden for men to take notice of women, and women of men, he is immediately attracted to her. Her name is Liberty 5-3000, but he thinks of her only as the Golden One. One day she comes close to the road and smiles at him. Every day after that they greet each other with their eyes. He realizes that he violates the law, which states that men may not think of women except for one night during the Time of Mating. He breaks another law on the day that he speaks to the Golden One. He tells her that she is beautiful, and she replies that he is not one of her brothers, for she does not wish him to be. Though their language has no concepts to explain her meaning, he understands, at an emotional level, that she is expressing the right of preference—that she holds him above and apart from all others as one who is special.

Although he does not understand why it should occur to him, he asks suddenly how old she is. She understands, for she is 17. Equality 7-2521 vows to himself that he will not permit her to be taken to the Palace of Mating. He does not know how he will prevent it, he knows only that he will.

He observes as he undresses at night that a feeling of fear hangs over the room, and no one is willing to speak what all seem to feel. He wonders, as he lies in bed at night, what the secrets were of the Unmentionable Times that have been lost. He thinks of what he has been taught: of the great fighting, in which many fought on one side and only a few on the other. He remembers that those few were the Evil Ones, and that they were destroyed along with all that was theirs. All the books of the Evils Ones were burned in the fires that raged across the land. Then came the Great Rebirth. But the words of the Unmentionable Times, he wonders. What were the words?

He knows that one word especially must not be re-discovered and said. It is called the Unspeakable Word, but nobody knows what it is. He has seen, as a boy, what fate befalls the rare person who discovers this word. He saw such a fellow burned at the stake after his tongue had been ripped from his mouth. Before the flames consumed him, Equality 7-2521 believes that the Transgressor looked at him, making eye contact, as if to pass on some holy knowledge that he alone possessed. What, he wonders, is the Unspeakable Word?

Commentary

In this chapter, Ayn Rand further develops Equality 7-2521's unconquerable independence of soul. In various aspects of life, he uncompromisingly follows his own mind rather than obeys the suppressive laws of the state. He refuses to ignore his growing love for Liberty 5-3000, though it is forbidden for men to notice women. He is attracted to her for reasons beyond her physical beauty, such as her straightness of backbone and fearless expression, outward signs of an independent spirit uncrushed by the stifling society in which she exists. Though they have had no more than eye contact and have not yet spoken, he knows immediately without words that they are kindred spirits.

Equality 7-2521's friendship with International 4-8818 and especially his love for the Golden One are choices based on preference. He values these two, for personal characteristics that each possesses, above other members of society. Even in a society as thoroughly collectivized as this, individuality is impossible to eradicate. Each individual is unique and unrepeatable, and myriad differences exist between and among them. Ayn Rand agrees with the American principle that individuals should be equal before the law, but this is the only sense in which they are equal. Morally and psychologically, they are different from one another, and some are better, some are worse. In *Anthem*, Rand shows Equality 7-2521 to have greater independence than his brothers and sisters. He refuses to bow and obediently follow in the way that most members of this society do. Similarly, International 4-8818 is willing to think for himself. He draws, against the rules and despite his punishment; he refuses to inform on Equality 7-2521 though his silence violates all the laws. The Golden One, with her head high and her eyes scornful, also reveals an uncompromising moral character that stands out in this society.

Theme

Human beings are not equal. They make different *choices*. Though many choose to accept and follow, some choose to think and live independently. The freethinking men and women of *Anthem* choose to have deeper, more intimate relationships with one another than with passive followers. They reject the egalitarianism of their society—the belief that all human beings should be treated as absolute equals—and live by the principle of individualism, choosing the men and women whom they value. In so doing, they refuse to permit personal values to perish from this earth.

Personal values are critical to understanding why members of this society are unhappy, why some cry for no apparent reason, and why others scream uncontrollably in the night. An individual's happiness depends on an ability to pursue and attain values, those things personally important to that individual. Equality 7-2521, who loves science, is joyous when beneath the ground pursuing the studies so meaningful to him. But this society stifles an individual's freedom to pursue personal values, so it is to be expected that its citizens experience life as meaningless and painful, which is why Fraternity cries, and Solidarity screams in the night. Consciously, they have no knowledge of individuality and personal values, but at an emotional level, they experience the drab dreariness of a life devoid of meaning. They suffocate in an airtight society and gasp for breath.

Equality 7-2521's independence is further shown in his wondering regarding the Unmentionable Times and, especially, the Unspeakable Word. These thoughts are strictly forbidden, and speaking them, punishable by death, but Equality 7-2521 is undaunted. His thirst for knowledge extends beyond scientific matters and includes questions of history and ethics. Regarding every important issue of life—science, morality, love—his is a freethinking mind eager to learn. Unlike his brothers, he is unafraid to explore and to ask questions that others would not dare to. His honest wondering about the Uncharted Forest foreshadows his bold decision to later flee there despite the dangers it presents to his life.

Literary Device

The role of the Saint of the Pyre here is important. The dying man sees in Equality 7-2521 exactly what his teachers and the Golden One sees—his height, his straightness of spine, his searching eyes. The transgressor recognizes his successor when he sees him, and exhorts him with his eyes not to surrender the independence of spirit that is uniquely his. This episode, too, hints at what is to come.

Glossary

eugenics a system for improving the human species through control of hereditary factors in mating.

pyre a pile on which a dead body is burned, as in a funeral rite.

Home of the Peasants place of residence for the women who toil in the fields outside of the city limits. Liberty 5-3000 lives here with the other women who engage in the work of farming.

Golden One name that Equality 7-2521 gives in his own mind to Liberty 5-3000. He gives her this name not merely because her hair is as golden as the sun but also because the straightness of her carriage and the fearlessness of her eyes cause her to stand out, to shine forth from the other women.

Time of Mating the period each spring when the state sends all men older than 20 and all women older than 18 to spend one night in the Palace of Mating. Babies are born every winter but are immediately taken from their mothers and raised by the state. The children never know who their parents are, and the parents do not know who their children are.

Palace of Mating the building where the state-controlled breeding occurs. Sex is prohibited in this society except under the authority of the government, which permits it only for purposes of procreation.

Council of Eugenics state agency that governs all sexual activity and procreation. Its members determine who will sleep with whom, based on the best interest of the state, not the happiness of the men and women involved. If all vestiges of individuality and personal choice are to be expunged, then the Council must be certain that the sexual partners have no attachment to, or feelings for, each other.

Uncharted Forest heavily wooded area just outside the city and extends for many miles in distance. Many such unexplored forests range across the land and are believed to have grown over the ruins of the cities of the Unmentionable Times.

Script Fire brief interval initiating the Great Rebirth following the defeat of the Evil Ones during which all books and writings were burned.

Unspeakable Word the word "I," outlawed in this society under threat of death. The political rulers, in seeking to forbid all aspects of individualism, recognize that it is not sufficient to ban the actions of a personal life, but must also eradicate all thoughts of one.

Chapter 3

Summary

In his research, Equality 7-2521 discovers a new force of nature. He uses this force, which he calls the "power of the sky," to build strange new devices. He roams through the tunnel, garnering everything from this remnant of the Unmentionable Times that he can—boxes with bars of metal, wires leading to globes of glass on the wall, and more. He does not understand these strange objects, but he studies them. He believes that the people of the Unmentionable Times understood this force of the sky, and that they had somehow harnessed it to power their devices. He believes that the objects he has found in the tunnel bear some relation to this power. He commits himself to understanding this power even though it means going against every thing he has been taught to believe by the Councils.

Commentary

The "power of the sky" is, of course, electricity. In his research, Equality 7-2521 has discovered the long lost knowledge of this energy that, as he accurately surmises, was known to thinkers of the Unmentionable Times. Given his relentless dedication to the acquisition of scientific knowledge, it comes as no surprise to learn that he intends to follow this course of study until he understands it completely. Equality 7-2521, in this regard, is akin to such pioneers of the electric age as Thomas Edison, Nikola Tesla, and George Westinghouse. Edison invented not only the lightbulb but also created the world's first electric lighting system. Tesla invented the alternating current motor, and Westinghouse hired him to adapt the motor for use in his power system, which was capable of transmitting electricity over greater distances than the then-dominant method employing direct current. Like these great thinkers of an earlier age, Equality 7-2521 is an innovator, a man who develops new ideas. Unlike them, he lives in a collectivist dictatorship that threatens his life for the "crime" of freethinking.

Equality 7-2521 is on his way to a discovery even more momentous than electricity. He moves painfully toward the realization that the independent mind is the highest value on earth and is capable of greater achievement than that dreamed of by the crowd of blind followers. "No single one can possess greater wisdom than the many Scholars," he reminds himself. And yet, "we can. We do. We have fought against saying it, but now it is said." Though belief in the superiority of the individual mind is held to be the cardinal sin in this society, Equality 7-2521 gropes toward recognizing its truth. He does not yet know that great innovators of history have often been opposed and tormented by their societies. He has no way of knowing that these great men and women were moved by dedication to their own visions, not by desire to serve humanity—but he feels it, he *lives* it, and he slowly comes to understand it. Equality 7-2521's battle involves more than a quest for scientific breakthroughs against a hostile society; it embodies the struggle of the independent mind to recognize its supreme value in a world bent on keeping this truth suppressed.

Glossary

loadstone a strongly magnetized rock, especially one containing magnetite; something that attracts, as with magnetic force.

Power of the Sky lightning that streaks the sky during thunderstorms. In fact, lightning is generated by a discharge of atmospheric electricity from one cloud to another or between a cloud and the earth. No one in this backwards society has an idea of the connection between lightning and electricity, or even of the existence of electricity as a force of nature.

Chapter 4

Summary

Many days pass before Equality 7-2521 speaks again to the Golden One. He tells her that, in his private thoughts, he does not think of her as Liberty 5-3000. She replies that she does not think of him as Equality 7-2521 and has also given him a personal name: The Unconquered. When he reminds her that such thoughts are forbidden, she answers that he thinks them and that he wishes her to do the same. "Yes," he whispered. "Our dearest one, do not obey us." She steps back, stunned at his words, her eyes wide. "Speak these words again," she says. "Our dearest one." Never, he thinks, have men said this to women.

Commentary

Equality 7-2521 and the Golden One discover the meaning of love in a society utterly devoid of it. Love, the author shows, is a response to *personal values*. Equality 7-2521, a scientist, is a thinker, a man who values his own independent judgment over the unthinking conformity of the crowd. He values this quality in others, such as his friend, Independence 4-8818, who draws, even though it is forbidden for all except those at the Home of the Artists. Similarly, he values the proud posture and haughty demeanor of the Golden One, because these outer characteristics indicate a spirit that refuses to obey. Her independence of spirit, even more than her physical beauty, attracts Equality 7-2521. Indeed, part of the beauty that shines in her face and from her eyes is the outward reflection of the freespiritedness that forms the essence of her character. Similarly, because her spirit is unbowed, she prizes this attribute in Equality 7-2521 and names him The Unconquered.

Character Insight

Equality 7-2521 values scientific research and the independent mind that conducts the quest for timeless truth. These are the values most important to him. And he loves both Liberty 5-3000 and Independence 4-8818 because they embody such independence in their characters. Only men and women who hold personal values are capable of loving. The herd of conformists, who have relinquished their minds to the state, are incapable of experiencing this profoundly personal emotion. Love involves an individual casting an inner verdict of "yes" on another man or woman. To pass such a judgment requires a strong sense of self and of what one considers personally important. The sad majority of persons in Equality 7-2521's society have had all sense of self drained from them by the state. Consequently, they exist in a loveless condition.

Glossary

The Unconquered   the secret name that the Golden One has given to Equality 7-2521 in the privacy of her own mind. She loves him because his straightness of spine and pride of bearing show that his soul has not been conquered by the state. His independence of spirit stands out in his demeanor, and the Golden One recognizes it.

Chapter 5

Summary

After countless nights of experimenting, Equality 7-2521 succeeds in harnessing the power of electricity to re-invent the electric light. It is light in a rudimentary form: A box of glass that glows when its wires are connected. This power can be harnessed to benefit society. But how is he to convince others of this great new boon?

He knows many will fear his discovery; worse, the authorities will be enraged at his transgression, at his daring to think and work alone. He believes the Scholars are the only ones who will understand and recognize the merit of his invention. When the World Council of Scholars convenes in his city, he will present to them, as his gift, the "glass box with the power of the sky." The Scholars will explain the value of the invention to the Council of Vocations, and it will reassign Equality 7-2521 to the Home of the Scholars.

A new thought strikes him: He cares, for the first time, what becomes of his body. He wonders, for the first time in his life, what he looks like. Men never see their own faces in this society, and are forbidden to ask their brothers. They have been taught that it is evil to have concern for their own faces and bodies. But now, for some reason he does not understand, he desires to see his face.

Commentary

Equality 7-2521 can be thought of as the Thomas Edison of his age, the man who discovers how to employ the power of electricity to generate light. But the conditions under which Equality 7-2521 conducts his research are vastly more difficult. He must sneak around, concealing his precious work as though it was a guilty secret. He has only three hours at night for his studies, after working all day as a Street Sweeper. He crouches alone in a dimly lit, ill-equipped tunnel. He forages and steals what supplies he can. He has nobody with whom to brainstorm and discuss his ideas. He receives no moral support from his society—only its opposite, the threat of punishment and death if caught. In short, the harsh conditions under which Equality 7-2521 carries out his work underscore an important truth regarding innovators: They are motivated solely by their love of the work.

Theme

Equality 7-2521 loves science. He burns with passion to study it and understand nature's secrets. Researchers and inventors follow their own vision, their own truth. Equality 7-2521 is pleased that his electric light will benefit society, but society's gain is not the primary motivating factor of his work. Rather, his own personal values impel him, the importance that he—alone among the members of this society—places on this creative work. Ayn Rand shows that creative work is *personal*, not *social*. When personal values are extirpated from an individual's life, he or she cannot engage in creative work.

As a consequence of holding and reaching values of his own, Equality 7-2521 experiences the previously unknown sensation of pride. When he gazes upon the wires glowing in the dark, he is filled with a sense of his accomplishment. He thinks of the wires as veins torn from his body. The invention is merely an extension of his self, something brought into existence by his mind and his hands. A powerful experience of self-love fills him—a creator's recognition of achievement and of the value possessed by the one who accomplishes it. This sense of self worth is why, for the first time, he desires to see his face and know what he looks like. The recognition of his inner beauty leads him to expect that his external demeanor will match it.

He recognizes that he and he alone created this invention—that it was his brain and his hands that brought the light into existence. He knows that his brothers contributed nothing but the obstacles. Equality 7-2521 moves one step closer to recognizing the reality of individuality, that human beings are not mere appendages of a faceless, social mass. Clearly to him, only one man invented the light—"we" did not accomplish it—and it enables him to further question his lifelong indoctrination by society. He is almost ready to throw off the tyranny of "we," and to discover the lost and sacred Unspeakable Word.

Glossary

The Box of Glass rudimentary form of an electric light that Equality 7-2521 has re-invented. Though he knows little about electricity, he recognizes that lightning is caused by the same force that generates the light.

Chapter 6

Summary

Equality 7-2521 is caught. On the night he completes his invention, he neglects to watch the hourglass that tells him the time. When he remembers to look at it, it is too late. When the members of the Home Council question him regarding his whereabouts, he answers: "We will not tell you." The Council sends him to the Palace of Corrective Detention, commanding that he be lashed until he confesses. He escapes from the Palace of Corrective Detention and steals quickly into his tunnel. When he lights his candle, he finds everything as he left it. The glass box is intact, and when he beholds it, he feels that the scars on his back are unimportant.

Commentary

A collectivist society is brutally repressive in its treatment of those who think independently. Just like it burned at the stake the Saint of the Pyre for discovering and uttering the Unspeakable Word, so it lashes Equality 7-2521 for his unexplained absence. In a Nazi or Communist society such as this, obedience is considered the fundamental virtue. Individualists, like Equality 7-2521, who act on their own thinking, are regarded as dangerous troublemakers and treated like criminals.

Equality 7-2521 knows that if the state discovers the full extent of his "crimes"—his illicit scientific research and invention of an electric light—he will be executed and his creation destroyed. He has performed actions that are major violations of the lock-step conformity required by society. He has placed the satisfaction of his own goals above the necessity of compliance to society—and this is unforgivable. The legal authorities will not understand the significance of the light nor will they care. They will see only the refusal to conform. Equality 7-2521's only hope lies with the Scholars. They are the men of wisdom. The Scholars, he believes, are honest seekers after truth, who will both understand and care about the electric light. They will intercede on his behalf—and he and the light will be saved.

Equality 7-2521's unyielding allegiance to his invention and his mind—his refusal to betray his secret activities—illustrates the integrity of the creative geniuses persecuted by society. Ayn Rand shows the blatant falsehood of the collectivists' claim to love humankind. If the Nazis and Communists were sincere, they would neither ban independent thinking nor punish the thinkers.

**Literary
Device**

The ease with which Equality 7-2521 escapes from prison illustrates two points. The first is that the technological decline is so thorough that even the locks on the doors are rusted and aged, unable to withstand applied pressure. The more important point is that the collectivist state has succeeded in so thoroughly inculcating obedience that it has no need to post guards in either the prison or on the city streets. Under the brainwashing they have received from birth, citizens do not regard themselves as individuals; they have no right to think, and their only reason to live is to obey and serve. It does not occur to them to think, to question, to challenge authority. The state has no need to maintain systematic vigilance, for an independent thinker such as Equality 7-2521 has not appeared in anyone's memory. The authorities are surprised by the one unexplained absence that they know of. When they discover the full extent of Equality 7-2521's illicit actions, they will be flabbergasted. Nobody has ever heard of such a thing.

Glossary

City Theater the large tent in which are performed plays for the social recreation of the workers. The plays are about the virtues of toil and the need to sacrifice oneself for one's brothers.

Palace of Corrective Detention the prison to which Equality 7-2521 is taken after he is discovered absent from the theater. The prison, as virtually everything in this backwards society, is delapidated, posing no difficulty to Equality 7-2521's escape when the time is right.

World Council of Scholars the society of thinkers and scientists made up supposedly of the world's greatest minds. But since the political rulers value only obedience, the best thinkers (like Equality 7-2521) are excluded, leaving the World Council filled with a group of unthinking conformists.

Chapter 7

Summary

In the morning, Equality 7-2521 slips through the streets carrying his glass box. He enters unquestioned the Home of the Scholars, walking through the empty corridors into the great hall where the Scholars sit assembled. When he greets them, Collective 0-0009, the oldest and wisest, responds with a question regarding his identity. Equality 7-2521 informs them that he is a Street Sweeper, and they are first astonished and then outraged. Equality 7-2521 interrupts by pointing out that he is unimportant. He has something to show them of great significance to society.

He places the glass box on the table and connects the wires. When the wires begin to glow red, terror strikes the members of the Council. They leap from the table and run to the farthest wall, where they huddle together. The Scholars are furious that he defies all the Councils by believing he can provide greater benefit to his fellow man than cleaning the streets. They berate him for holding thoughts that are individual in opposition to those held by his brothers. They threaten him with torture and execution.

Equality 7-2521 pleads with them. He states that they are right regarding him. He is a miserable wretch who has broken all the laws, and who deserves only punishment. But the light, he questions. What will they do with the light? They smile and ask him if his brothers agree that the light is a great advance. When he admits that they do not, they point out that what is not believed by all men cannot be true. When they reiterate that he has worked on the invention alone, he concedes that he has. They remind him that what is not shared by all cannot be good. Other scholars argue that if the light is everything Equality 7-2521 claims, then it would ruin the Department of Candles; and since the candle is a benefit that has been approved by all men, its manufacture cannot be ended to satisfy the whim of one. It took 50 years to secure approval for the candle from all the Councils, to determine the number needed and to adjust from torches. The Plans of the World Councils cannot be changed again so soon. The World Council of Scholars decides in unison that the light must be destroyed.

Before they can touch the light, Equality 7-2521 seizes it and leaps through the window. He flees blindly, running through the streets of the city with no destination, knowing merely that he must get away. Suddenly, he finds himself on the soft earth, surrounded by trees taller than he's ever seen, and realizes that he is in the Uncharted Forest. Alone in the Forest, he believes he is doomed, that he will be devoured by ravenous beasts. He draws strength only from the box in his arms, realizing that he made it not for the sake of his brothers but for its own sake. His only regret is that he will not see the Golden One again. He thinks that because he is damned, it is best for her that she forgets him and everything about him.

Commentary

Equality 7-2521's innocent confidence that the Scholars will understand and support his invention of the light is misplaced. Equality 7-2521's commitment to research, to science, and to the independent mind causes him to admire humans, to respect the "rational animal." He still expects humans to be rational. He is a Humanist, one who holds that human life and well-being is the highest value on earth. Despite the horrors of life in his society, he still believes that the authorities are committed to human life. He thinks that the collectivists are sincere in their claims to love humankind. Because the benefit to society that is represented by the electric light is very clear, he expects the Scholars to recognize and support it. He does not yet understand the evil of the collectivists. His interview with the Scholars is a turning point in his thinking.

Ayn Rand shows that the collectivist authorities do not care about the light or the benefits it will bring; they desire neither inventions nor prosperity. What they do desire is obedience. Earlier, as Equality 7-2521 worked on harnessing electricity, he had realized that the Scholars do not know the things he knows. But at that time, he still believed that they *cared*. He believed that when laid before them, they would recognize the great benefit the light represents. Now he sees them reject the light. Clearly, the scholars know that the light is real, not a fantasy; it works. They know the power is harnessed and under control, not a raging threat. They recognize the light's potential. They all but concede that it will put the candle out of business. Rather, they do not *want* the light. They do not want the light because they fear its source: the independent mind. They fundamentally repudiate a man who thinks for himself and who refuses to conform to society.

Theme

To maintain the dictatorship, everyone must unquestioningly obey the Councils. Those who refuse to obey are a threat. Independent thinkers are a danger to this repressive society.

More important than the technological upheaval is the political one. Independent thinkers ask questions of humanity, as well as of nature. They want to understand the moral basis of a tyrant's regime as fully as they seek to comprehend the power of electricity. Great minds are not turned off when they leave the laboratory. They continue to ask questions and to seek truth. They question the moral legitimacy of the state.

Equality 7-2521 already has disturbing questions. He wonders about the Unspeakable Word, the lost secrets of the Unmentionable Times, why his brothers cry out in the night, and more. If the collectivists permit him to act on his own thinking, he will be more than an individual troublemaker; he will be an example to others. Other individuals who seek to think for themselves—such as the Golden One, who breaks the laws by speaking to Equality 7-2521, and International 4-8818, who draws on walls in defiance of the rules—will be encouraged to do so. If Equality 7-2521 is permitted to escape harsh punishment for his "crimes," much less be accepted as a great inventor, then the iron grip that the collectivists hold on society will be gravely undermined. The authorities recognize this, and cannot permit it to happen. Worse for them, in this scene Equality 7-2521 begins to recognize it, too.

He does not yet know what is the proper political system for men, nor does he explicitly understand the deeper causes of the collectivists' evil. But he knows that they reject the light, and that there is no place for him in such a society. He fully expects to die in the forest. But even that is preferable to life as an unthinking slave in the city.

Chapter 8

Summary

Equality 7-2521's first day in the forest is astonishing to him. His first impulse is to leap to his feet as he has every day of his life, but then he realizes that no bell has rung. The forest has no Councils to tell him what to do, no authorities that must be instantly obeyed. He experiences joy when he realizes that no activity is denied him any longer.

For the first time in his 21 years, he is free. He walks with no destination, but not aimlessly; he enjoys the freedom of movement. He keeps walking and comes upon a stream. When he kneels to drink, he stops. For the first time, on the water before him, he sees the reflection of his face. He notices the taut lines of his body and the countenance that arouses no pity. In this regard, his face and body are unlike those of his brothers. Theirs are bowed and defeated, evoking in him a general sense of pity. But his features are straight and healthy, generating the feeling of pride. He realizes that he can trust this man he sees before him in the stream; he has nothing to fear.

Commentary

For anyone, the first day of freedom is exhilarating. For Equality 7-2521, who has been subjugated in a slave society for 21 years, the right to pursue his own happiness is akin to the first bite of food to a starving man. For the first time, he can do as he pleases and is not subject to the commands of the Councils. He spends his first day of freedom discovering his body and its capabilities. He climbs a tree, hunts and cooks his own food, sees the image of his face for the first time. This pleasure is far more than that of someone enjoying the luxury of a hard-earned vacation; it is the exploration of a man released from a lifelong imprisonment, free now to discover himself. His time in the forest is a voyage. In one way, he journeys physically from one place to another—from the city to the home he eventually finds in the mountains. But in a more profound way, he travels a long path of self-discovery, and he learns quickly. He has been limited to sweeping the streets, but now he engages in hundreds of different activities and learns his own diverse abilities.

Theme

Ayn Rand believes in the heroic potential of humans. Although Equality 7-2521 has never hunted game or cooked a meal, he is a rational man and possesses the capacity to learn. Human beings have often reached difficult goals under arduous circumstances. They have circumnavigated the globe, traversed the polar ice caps, and climbed Mt. Everest. Individuals with less genius and will to live than Equality 7-2521 have survived emergencies and catastrophes. Equality 7-2521's willingness to face all dangers and to learn new skills reminds us of the human potential. Long ago, Aristotle defined humankind as the rational animal, and Equality 7-2521—inventor, independent thinker—is an example of how much a rational man is able to accomplish by use of his own mind.

Character Insight

That Equality 7-2521 sees his face for the first time is significant. He is not one of the faceless masses who blends into the multitudes of society. He is an exceptional man who stands forth from the crowd. He, by virtue of his independence, has created his own unique identity. Appropriately, he recognizes his differences from the other members of society. He thinks and acts differently; therefore he looks differently. Where others have allowed their souls to be conquered and stand with bowed spine, he has maintained his independence and walks erect. Upon seeing his reflection for the first time, he takes an important step on the path to self-discovery: he recognizes that his willingness to think—his inner difference—results in an outer difference as well. An individual's appearance is not an utterly distinct matter from his inner reality. Equality 7-2521's integrity—his refusal to surrender his mind to society—shows in his posture, his movements, and his eyes.

The Golden One recognizes these outer manifestations of his spirit and approves—she is drawn to him. The Councils also recognize them, but disapprove; they punish him. Now Equality 7-2521, too, sees the unmistakable differences between himself and others. His quiet shock at his own outer beauty drives home to him what he already knows: He is a man of great strength of character. He continues writing his thoughts, just as he did when alone in the tunnel. He has made progress, but there is still so much that he does not comprehend. He searches for the words to understand. This dedication to knowledge is what sets him apart.

Chapter 9

Summary

On his second day in the forest, Equality 7-2521 hears steps behind him. When the steps come closer, he recognizes the form of the Golden One. She is too overcome initially to speak, but he asks how she came to be in the forest. She says that she followed him and tells him that the whole city speaks of his escape. On the night of the day she heard of his escape, she fled from the Home of the Peasants, entered the forest, and followed the trail he had left. Her tunic is torn and her skin is cut, but she takes no notice of either. She is not afraid. She tells him that she will go where he goes, that she will face the dangers he faces and share the fate that befalls him. If he dies, then she will die with him. She says he may do as he pleases with her, but he must not send her away. She kneels before him.

Equality 7-2521 does not understand what happens next. He bends to raise her to her feet, but when his skin touches hers it is "as if madness had stricken us." He takes her in his arms, presses his lips to hers and she wraps her arms around him. They stand together for a long time, and he is frightened that he has lived for 21 years without knowing the joy that is possible to men.

That night they make love, and he discovers that to hold a woman in his arms is "the one ecstasy granted to the race of men."

But even in his newfound happiness he asks disturbing questions. If this solitude of theirs is evil, he wonders, then what kind of happiness is possible to human beings? If this is wrong, as they have been taught all their lives, then what is right? Now for the first time, he begins to doubt the truth of this teaching.

One day the Golden One says to him, "We love you. " But she frowns and shakes her head, realizing that those words—that word, "we"—do not capture the truth of her feelings. He looks into her eyes, knowing that for one instant they had been on the verge of a discovery. But then the instant flees. He wonders, what is the word that they lack?

Commentary

Ayn Rand continues her theme of independent thinking and personal values in another form. The Golden One, like Equality 7-2521, has been taught that life's meaning lies exclusively in selfless toil for her brothers and sisters. At a conscious level, she accepts the only beliefs she has ever heard. But implicitly, she does not agree. She is drawn to Equality 7-2521 because of his unconquered soul. He—and the independence he represents—is what she wants out of life, and all the teachings of the collectivists are powerless to change her mind. Though the result is damnation and execution if she is caught, she will not be denied. She refuses to surrender her love. Against all the beliefs of her society, she flees the city and pursues Equality 7-2521 through the Uncharted Forest.

Character Insight

The Golden One understands at some wordless level that human beings must conduct life in accordance with their own judgment, and that life's meaning lies in the attainment of personal values. *She* loves Equality 7-2521 and everything he stands for, regardless of what her brothers and sisters believe. If she is to be happy, then she must be true in action to her convictions. In the heroine's character, as well as the hero's, the author shows that the meaning of life lies in values that are *personal*, not *social*, in things and goals that are uniquely and distinctively one's own.

Love is one such value. Because human beings are denied individuality in this society, they know no love. The state understands that love is *preference*, the valuing of one individual over all others. To stamp out individuality, the collectivist authorities must forbid love, which is why procreation is controlled by the state. In deciding who sleeps with whom and when, the authorities ensure that men and women are prohibited from making choices based on their own values. Equality 7-2521 and the Golden One discover love as a consequence of their commitment to their selves. They think for themselves, judge for themselves, and choose for themselves. The depth of love they hold for each other is a direct result of their recognition that human beings are unique individuals, not interchangeable parts of a whole.

The romantic love experienced by Equality 7-2521 and the Golden One is not shared with the rest of humankind. Love is a function of the self. Everything Equality 7-2521 is—his genius, his inventiveness, his relentless pursuit of truth—comes from his independence. This essence of *him*—of his self, of his soul—is what draws the proud, unconquered spirit of this beautiful young woman. She stands out from her sisters regarding the exact virtues that cause Equality 7-2521 to stand out from his brothers. They choose each other, and they choose in accordance with their own values, not in compliance with society's laws or customs. Their love is personal, a function of the deepest convictions of their individual souls. This is the nature of romantic love, according to Rand.

Equality 7-2521's quest for knowledge is also personal. Society disapproves of the questions he asks regarding both science and philosophy. His passion for truth drives him. His is the mind of a great thinker, determined to understand, fearless regarding the consequences. He seeks to discover the Unspeakable Word though it means certain death if he is caught. Rand shows that great scientists and thinkers such as Equality 7-2521 are driven by their own vision, their own passion for knowledge, despite the antipathy of society. They are on a relentless quest generated by a love of wisdom they possess deep in their souls.

Style & Language

His attempt to identify the Unspeakable Word—the forbidden thought that would explain so much—comes close to fruition. The Golden One, struggling with the same idea, expresses herself haltingly: "We are one . . . alone . . . and only . . ." They look at each other then, knowing that "the breath of a miracle had touched" them. But then the moment was gone, leaving them with the aching awareness that some vital component of knowledge was still denied them.

Chapter 10

Summary

Equality 7-2521 and the Golden One discover a house in the depths of the forest, a house such as they have never seen resting on a broad summit with the mountains behind it. The house has two stories, a flat roof, and walls made more of glass than of any other substance. They immediately understand that no one they know built this structure. The house is a remnant of the Unmentionable Times.

Equality 7-2521 realizes that they will need years to understand all that they find in the house. They are surprised by the smallness of the rooms and decide that no more than 12 men could have occupied them. When they come to the bedroom and find only two beds, they are baffled by the recognition that this building was home to but two persons. They find clothes that are not limited to white tunics or togas, but are of diverse colors and styles. They encounter mirrors, and Equality 7-2521 notices on the walls the same globes of wire-filled glass that he had seen in his tunnel. He is amazed when he comes to the library and finds shelves of books. He ascertains that they are written in their language and decides that the next day he will begin to read them.

When they look at all of the house's rooms, Equality 7-2521 says to the Golden One that the house is theirs. It belongs to them alone; they will not leave or allow it to be taken from them. He says that they will not share it with others in the sense that they do not share their love or their joy or their hunger. The Golden One agrees.

That night Equality 7-2521 does not sleep. He senses that the earth awaits his command, that in some way he and the Golden One are to give it "its goal, its highest meaning." He does not know what word he is to speak or what deed he is to perform. He knows only that the final fulfillment of the earth's promise must come from him and those like him, but he lacks the knowledge necessary to bring these great deeds to pass. What is the secret, he wonders, that his heart has grasped but his mind is yet to comprehend?

Commentary

Their discovery of a home surviving from the Unmentionable Times is significant because it links them in physical action, as well as in spirit, to the attainments of the lost era. Equality 7-2521 had intended to build a home, which would be a great accomplishment. But a home that he would build would not express the kinship existing between him and the freethinkers of the past who had reached such lofty achievements. By finding and occupying a home from the forgotten era, Equality 7-2521 and the Golden One not only derive practical benefits from the lost advances but also immerse themselves in the world they seek to re-create. The great thinker who re-invents electric light links himself inextricably with the independent thinkers of the past who originally created it.

Equality 7-2521 realizes that the books in the home can provide the knowledge possessed by those of the Unmentionable Times, secrets lost for centuries. His decision to study the books is a continuation of his crusade to gain both scientific understanding of nature and a moral and philosophical understanding of humankind. His research into the "power of the sky" and his harnessing of electricity to create light are obvious examples of his scientific discoveries. But his philosophizing is of even greater importance. He is one of the few in his society, like the executed Saint of the Pyre, who searches for the Unspeakable Word and for the precious knowledge represented by this word.

Character Insight

Equality 7-2521's noblest quality (which will result in his greatest achievement) is his unflinching quest to rediscover the individualistic nature of man and the political liberty that such a nature requires. Against every type of social opposition, he persists in this endeavor until, in this chapter, with the books at his disposal of those who understood these sacred truths, he stands on the threshold of the wisdom he seeks. He is as great a philosopher as he is a scientist. The books of the individualistic, capitalist past will give him the knowledge denied to those in his collectivist present.

Chapter 11

Summary

"I am. I think. I will." So opens the chapter in which Equality 7-2521 re-discovers the lost and holy word, the forbidden idea for which the Saint of the Pyre was burned at the stake. The acquisition of this knowledge fulfills the intellectual quest on which Equality 7-2521 had embarked as a 10-year-old—the attempt to discover and understand the Unspeakable Word.

He had searched for meaning in life, and now realizes that he is the meaning. He had wished to find a warrant for being, but now understands that he needs neither warrant nor sanction. He is the warrant and sanction of his existence. He is overcome with the emotional experience of his intellectual realization: he has a right to his own life. He is not a mere appendage of a group. He can choose his own path in life—his own interests, his own profession, his own wife, his own home. He is a free man, able to choose his goals, and then work strenuously to achieve them. Related to this is his realization that no individual—neither himself nor any other human being—is a tool to be employed by others for some end they seek to accomplish. Humans are not servants, he claims, to bow and scrape before society, to render obedient service. An individual is "not a sacrifice on their altars."

Equality 7-2521 realizes, after studying the books of the Unmentionable Times, what the proper relation is between individuals. He owes no unchosen obligations to his brothers and sisters, nor do they owe him such. He states that he is neither a friend nor a foe to others, "but such as each of them shall deserve." Love, he claims, must be earned—and that requires more than the sheer fact of being born; it requires the attainment of virtue.

Equality 7-2521 will choose friends from among his fellow humans, but neither masters nor servants. He says that he will love and respect his friends, but neither command nor obey them. And when humans come together in friendship and in love, they will join hands only beyond each one's "holy threshold," and each will respect the personal boundaries of the other. Looking back on his past life in the city—and thinking sorrowfully of those innocent people still trapped there—

he realizes that the horrors of his former society are the result of destroying the personal boundaries that each individual properly claims as their own. Equality 7-2521 proclaims that he is forever done with the code of "we," with this creed of evil and destruction. He sees clearly the beneficent consequences that can result—as they did in the past—when society recognizes the sacred rights of individuals to mind, soul, values, and life. He observes the face of a god, the god sought by humans since the inception of the world, the god who will grant joy and peace and pride. "This god, this one word: I."

Commentary

Equality 7-2521 has learned more than the word "I" from studying the texts of the Unmentionable Times. He has begun to understand the individualistic philosophy that underlies the meaning and value of this word. Equality 7-2521 had always understood this philosophy implicitly—he had felt that it was true and had lived it in action. But prior to the events of this chapter, he had not the conceptual understanding of such a philosophy; he lacked the vocabulary—the very words—necessary to think about it. In reading the lost books, he discovers the words and the thoughts that explain and validate what he has always felt. At the emotional level, he had always believed an individual has the right to his own life. Now, for the first time, he knows this is true, understanding it as an explicit, fully articulated intellectual theory.

Style & Language

The emotional power of this chapter must be noted. Leading to this point in the story have been pages of unrelenting collectivism. The reader has been immersed in a world in which all shreds of individuality have been ruthlessly extirpated, in which the word "we" is the only form of first-person reference known, and in which the group holds unquestioned dominion over an individual's life. Now, as Equality 7-2521 opens the chapter with the words, "I am, I think, I will," the impact of those words is profound. Equality 7-2521 has been liberated in a way far more fundamental than his physical escape. He is finally freed from the collectivist philosophy with which he has been indoctrinated all his life.

Formerly, the collectivist state owned his mind, for he still accepted the truth of their principles. Even in his acts of rebellion—during his scientific research when hidden in his tunnel, when illicitly wooing the Golden One, as he made his escape into the Uncharted Forest—he still believed that what he did was wrong. He still thought of himself as a transgressor worthy of punishment. He had rejected the collectivist code emotionally and in action. He had asked questions and tried to understand. But given his necessarily limited amount of knowledge, he had not the capacity to reach a full level of comprehension. When he reads the books of those of the lost times, however, he acquires the vocabulary of freedom. His opening words of the chapter have all the meaning and emotional power of his final liberation from slavery.

Theme

The fundamental purpose of this chapter is to explain what the events of the book have dramatized. The story has already shown that the subordination of the individual to the group leads to nothing but destruction in human life. Now Ayn Rand, through the intellectual discoveries of the hero, provides a philosophical explanation. The "I," Equality 7-2521 understands, represents the fundamental truth about a human being's nature. A human's mind and spirit are personal attributes; they do not belong to others and are not communal property. A person's innermost thoughts—hopes, dreams, values, aspirations, loves—belong exclusively to that person. These thoughts are the priceless items that give life its meaning and are not to be seized by others for any purpose whatever. If the content of a person's mind is to be dictated by the state, then no human life is possible, only the existence of a worker ant in unrelenting toil to the colony. The "I," or self, is sacred and must be preserved at all costs.

The "we," or group, can be a positive force in humanity, but only when it is understood to be a derivative phenomenon. Human beings can form a society beneficial to all of its members only when they recognize the sovereign right of each individual to his or her own life. Equality 7-2521 knows full well what it is like when society does not recognize this truth—indeed, he has had the lesson taken out on his hide. When the individual is denied this basic right, all that is then possible is a slave society.

But Equality 7-2521 now understands that if society recognizes individuality, then benevolent interaction in numerous forms becomes possible. Clearly, persons who respect each other's rights and boundaries can bond in close friendships of the kind between Equality 7-2521 and International 4-8818. Similarly, if human beings recognize the unique and distinctive characteristics of each individual, then they are capable of romantic love, such as the relationship between Equality 7-2521 and the Golden One. Recognition of each person's unrepeatable attributes of selfhood makes it possible to choose, to value, to have preferences.

Friendship and love are both discriminatory. They are preferential and not given equally to all comers. The feelings of friendship and love that give rise to close human relationships are selective responses given only to rare individuals who embody in their lives and persons the qualities that the chooser values. Such individualized responses are not possible in a society so collectivized that all recognition of individuality is expunged from thinking. Friendship, love, and valuing are functions of the self. All these inner actions are performed exclusively by individuals, not by groups; these actions are personal, not social, in nature. Societies, Equality 7-2521 now realizes, are merely groups of individuals. Societies are secondary manifestations; the individual is fundamental.

Further, although Equality 7-2521's study of his ancient texts of individuality and freedom may not be sufficiently advanced to give him knowledge of economics, a further benefit to humankind exists from living in a society that recognizes and respects individual personhood: a division of labor economy. For when individuals have "inalienable rights," as one of the writers of that ancient civilization proclaimed, then they are free to choose their own interests, including their professions. When individuals pursue the careers they love, as Equality 7-2521 does with scientific research, they are motivated, even to the point of crouching in a hidden tunnel to gain several precious hours alone for their studies. Persons with that degree of incentive are significantly more productive than those whom the state forces into an occupation. As individuals with rights, they are willing to work longer and harder, for they both love their work and keep its proceeds. Such a free, capitalistic economy is far more prosperous than the collectivist dictatorship under which Equality 7-2521 formerly existed. As Equality 7-2521 studies further, he no doubt will gain these insights into economics. They are applications of what he has recently learned: that only when society realizes that each one is a sovereign individual with rights not to be abridged by the group, does life in human society become fulfilling. In the absence of this knowledge, all live under the oppressive tyranny of the collective.

The name of the moral theory that Equality 7-2521 has struggled to reach, and finally understands in this chapter, is *egoism*. The root word, ego, means "self" or "I." The theory of egoism states that individuals should be the beneficiaries of their own actions, should strive to attain their own happiness, and should not sacrifice the self. The code that Equality 7-2521 re-discovers, and that is endorsed by the author, is known as *rational egoism*. This theory holds that an individual should *earn* the things on which happiness depends. By means of education, hard work, and honest effort, persons should strive to reach those goals that will make them happy. Rational egoism rejects the victimization of others as a means of reaching happiness; it is a theory upholding the right of *all* individuals to work diligently and earn the things that bring meaning and joy into their lives.

When the moral code of rational egoism is applied to politics, it leads to a system of limited, constitutional government that protects an individual's inalienable right to life, liberty, and the pursuit of happiness. The ethics of rational egoism leads to a politics of individualism. Equality 7-2521 understands by means of his reading that, in the past, the moral code of rational egoism was expounded by some thinkers and led to political freedom for millions of individuals. This moral code and its political consequence are what Equality 7-2521 seeks to revive in his society.

Theme

In Equality 7-2521's society, egoism is considered evil and has been expunged over the centuries from its memory. In its place, society has taught an opposite code—the theory of *altruism*. Altruism states that individuals have a moral obligation to sacrifice themselves for others, that satisfying the desires of other persons should take precedence in an individual's life. Under this moral code, an individual has no right to his or her own life but exists solely as a servant of others.

When an altruist moral code is applied to politics, it leads to an individual's enforced servitude to society. On this view, an individual has no inalienable rights, but exists solely to serve the state. Just as a moral code of rational egoism leads directly to a politics of individualism and freedom, so the morality of altruism leads to a politics of collectivism and dictatorship. Equality 7-2521's reading teaches him that the widespread acceptance of altruism is what makes possible the horrors of the collectivist dictatorship he has recently escaped. Equality 7-2521 seeks to liberate his society from this moral code and its ensuing politics of slavery.

Equality 7-2521's education now includes an intellectual understanding of the moral code by which he will live, and the code he will shun. He understands that egoism is a code leading to *benevolence*, an attitude of kindness and goodwill toward others. He sees from his own life, as well as from his study of the free societies of the past, that when persons are encouraged to live their own lives, they are fulfilled and happy within themselves. Because they do not have to sacrifice themselves for others, people are no threat to them. Each has a right to self-fulfillment, so each, therefore, has value. The rational egoist, Equality 7-2521 now grasps, recognizes that human beings have rights and treats them accordingly—with respect and goodwill. Kindness toward others depends on the recognition that each individual possesses inalienable rights.

Additionally, based on the brutality of the collectivist society he has escaped, Equality 7-2521 realizes the horror of the altruist code. When persons have no rights—when they exist solely to serve the state—then they become just so many sacrificial animals. The code of self-sacrifice leads inevitably to slavery. In spite of their claims to human love, those who advocate human sacrifice have no love for human beings. If they did, they would not urge the surrender of personal values and the sacrifice of the self to the group. Rather, they would urge all to pursue their values, to achieve them, and to reach a state of joyous fulfillment. The code of rational egoism that Equality 7-2521 plans to offer will lead humankind to personal success and happiness. The code of altruism from which he hopes to deliver them leads only to slavery and misery.

Chapter 12

Summary

Equality 7-2521 says that when, in the course of his reading, he first discovered and understood the meaning of the word "I," he wept—he who had never known tears.

Equality 7-2521 reads many books for many days. When he finally lays aside his studies, he calls the Golden One and tells her what he has learned. Her first words on hearing his discoveries are: "I love you." He tells her that the code of individualism requires each person to have their own name to differentiate them from the rest of humankind. He tells her of a figure about whom he has read. He was a legendary hero who lived far in the past, who took the light of the gods and brought it to humans. In this way, "he taught men to be gods." He suffered for his deeds as all bearers of light must suffer. His name was Prometheus. "It shall be your name," replies the Golden One. Additionally, he tells her of a heroine from the legends of the past. She was a goddess who was the mother of the earth and of all the gods. Her name was Gaea. He requests that the Golden One take this name, for she is to be the mother of a new kind of gods. The Golden One agrees.

Prometheus looks ahead and sees the future clearly before him. Prometheus says that he will continue to live in his own house and learn to grow food by tilling the soil. He will gain much knowledge from his books and use that knowledge in the coming years to re-create the achievements of the past. He is proud of the attainments he can reach, but also saddened by the inability of others to do the same, for their minds are shackled by the collectivist philosophy that keeps them enslaved.

Prometheus learns that the power of the sky was known to the free-thinkers of the past; they called it electricity and used it to light their cities, heat their homes, and power their inventions. He has found the engine in the home that produces this power and will learn to repair it. He will study the wires that carry this power, learn how to use them, and then create a network of wires around his house and the paths that lead to his house. In this way, he will make the house impregnable from assault by others, for they have nothing with which to threaten him but their numbers. They use brute force, but he uses his mind.

Prometheus and Gaea will live on their mountaintop in peace and security. He says that she is pregnant with his child, who will be raised as a free man. Their son will be taught the word "I" and will learn reverence for his own spirit. He will learn what pride there is in being a human individual. When Prometheus's work is accomplished—when he has read the books, fortified their home, and tilled the soil—he intends to stealthily venture for the last time into the city of his birth. There he will call to him all those of independent spirit who remain—his friend International 4-8818 and all those like him. He will seek out Fraternity 2-5503, who cries without reason, and Solidarity 9-6347, who screams in the night. He will reach out to any of the men and women whose heads are still unbowed, who retain the slightest spark of autonomy and who yearn in some form for freedom. These individuals will flock to him, and they will return to his fortress. Prometheus says that here, in the uncharted wilderness, they will build their city and write a new chapter in the history of human freedom.

Commentary

Literary Device

That the hero and heroine take new names is significant for several reasons. They reject the collectivist names that were imposed on them by the slave society in which they were raised. The name Equality 7-2521 stands for a particular aspect of collectivist thinking. The collectivists do not mean by the term "equality" the individualistic principle that all individuals possess the same legal rights and are to be treated identically by the law. The collectivists mean that all are equal in an absolute sense—that no individual is or should be better than the crowd, that no one possesses greater talent than others or greater intelligence or greater virtue. It is the equality of an ant colony, in which all individuals are equally subordinated to and enslaved by the rulers.

The collectivists seek to prevent individuals from rising, from attaining excellence, from standing out, from achieving pride in their own person and accomplishments. Individuals free to live their lives and actualize their potential—who hold high standards in all areas of life and strive to consistently meet them—are not readily malleable by an all-powerful state. Such individuals do not conform or obey. They are independent, living by their own thinking, pursuing their own values, striving for their own happiness. But others taught that they have no right to rise above the herd, that they must seek no distinction, that each is the same as all, such unfortunates will bow and kneel and follow. Believing themselves no more than a cog in a vast machine, they will seek no individuality and will be ready clay for their masters to mold. The hero rejects this philosophy of humanity, and consequently rejects the name that embodies it.

Further, the numbers that follow every person's name are a means by which the rulers instill the same collectivist lesson. A human being is not an individual, according to the collectivist philosophy; he is merely a fragmented part of a greater whole. Mandating that numbers follow each name, in amounts running to four or five digits, signifies that each person is only one of thousands bearing the same name, belonging to the same tribe, serving the same group. No one person is unique, unrepeatable, or outstanding. She is merely a numbered and controlled member of society, a splintered part of which the group is the whole. The numbers and the collectivist names combine with the eradication of the word "I" to form a collectivist culture designed to extirpate even the knowledge of individuality. The hero and heroine, as an act symbolizing their commitment to an individualistic philosophy, must repudiate the practice of attaching numbers to a person's name.

Style & Language

Further, even though the Golden One's given name is Liberty 5-3000, the word "liberty" is so corrupted by the collectivists that it stands for the exact opposite of its original meaning. In the collectivist culture, liberty means not the inalienable right of each person to sovereign individuality, but rather the "right" of each person to be subordinate to the group. The collectivists, in their attempt to create universal slavery, corrupt the language—the very ideas and terms with which persons think—so as to obliterate all thoughts that clash with their push for blind obedience. The very concepts of individualism and freedom are expropriated and used to designate meanings that are the polar opposite of their originals. George Orwell, in his famous book, *1984*, shows the collectivist dictators similarly corrupting the vocabulary of liberty by making such irrational claims as "Freedom is slavery." Prometheus and Gaea, at this point in the story, finally understand the full evil of collectivism and repudiate all its forms and trappings, including the bastardized name originally given the Golden One. As befitting free individuals, they will choose their own names.

From studying his books, Prometheus has learned a good deal about the history of the Unmentionable Times. Although no specific historical details are given, it is reasonable to infer that he is knowledgeable regarding the ideas of the eighteenth century Enlightenment and the creation of the United States. He says that breaking free of the bonds imposed by various tyrants, persons of past eras "declared to all his brothers that a man has rights," and so "stood on the threshold of the freedom for which the blood of the centuries past had been spilled." Prometheus here refers to the ideas of such seventeenth- and eighteenth-century thinkers as John Locke and Voltaire, who argued that rational beings owed blind obedience to neither church nor state, but possessed the right to direct the course of their own life. Prometheus also has in mind men such as Thomas Jefferson, James Madison, and the other thinkers of America's founding period, who wrote the Declaration of Independence, the United States Constitution, and the Bill of Rights. The men responsible for the founding of the American republic were individualists who believed that the only moral purpose of government was to protect the right of individual citizens to pursue their own happiness. Clearly, from his brief commentary, Prometheus has learned these important facts of history and greatly admires these freedom fighters of the past.

Further, Prometheus now knows the history of collectivism's development in the nineteenth and twentieth centuries. Although he does not mention the specific historical details, his readings will have informed him of the work of the German philosophers G.W.F. Hegel and Karl Marx, whose writings proclaimed the superiority of the nation and/or the working class to the individual. Hegel and Marx stressed the moral obligation of the individual to be subordinate to the needs of the group—and it was largely their teachings that led to the rise of National Socialism in Germany, to Communism in the Soviet Union, and to Fascism in Italy, the context in which Rand wrote *Anthem*. Prometheus understands that as the collectivist doctrines spread around the globe, they eventually swallowed the free countries and turned them into totalitarian dictatorships as well. In this fictional universe created by the author, the doctrine of individual rights died in countries such as the United States because humans were gradually taught to worship the word "we" and renounce their reverence for the word "I." But Prometheus, like some Thomas Jefferson of the future, does not intend to permit the spirit of freedom to die out on the earth. It is not enough that he, his family, and his friends will live in freedom on their protected mountaintop. He intends to rekindle the battle for individual rights, to challenge the global collectivist state, and to initiate a new revolution on behalf of political freedom. Prometheus will bring more than electric light to his society; he will provide something of far greater value than that. He will bring the light of freedom back into human lives after centuries of absence.

Prometheus is confident about the ultimate triumph of individualism and freedom over collectivism. The most important consideration regards the role of the mind in human life. Because the collectivists value blind obedience above all, they necessarily view the freethinking mind as their most dangerous foe. Independent thinkers like Prometheus have their own ideas and arrive at their own conclusions by a process of logical thought. *They hold their own minds as sacred,* enabling them to discover new truths in the field of electricity, or in biology, physics, medicine, music, philosophy, and so on. Free minds like these do not confine their judgment to issues in the professional fields they choose; they think also on moral and political issues and recognize the grave injustices of the collectivist dictatorship. They speak out on behalf of an individual's rights and in defense of political freedom.

Theme

Thinkers such as Prometheus represent a profound threat to the unquestioned authority of the collectivist leaders. For this reason, collectivists are ruthless in stamping out any hint or vestige of independence in their subjects. Because the authorities recognized the precociousness of Prometheus's intellect, not in spite of it, they consigned him in his youth to the profession of Street Sweeper, denying him the logical choice of being a Scholar. Because the collectivists stifle the mind, they have lost all elements of scientific and technological progress, including in the realm of military weapons. They are utterly primitive in all areas of their lives.

Prometheus knows this. He knows too that he and his wife and friends are nothing like this. They are men and women of the mind. Prometheus always knew implicitly that it was by means of independent thinking that humans survive and prosper on earth; this is why he was always fascinated by the "science of things," and why he defied all laws and rules to experiment alone in his tunnel. Now, after his reading regarding the accomplishments of the freethinkers of the past—given his knowledge of their "steel towers, flying ships and power wires"—he knows explicitly the importance of the mind. He and his friends will use the supreme power of their minds to defend themselves. Prometheus already plans to study the generator by means of which electric power in his home was formerly produced. He will learn to repair or replicate it. His study of electrical engineering will, in the future, enable him to create new products of immense use to his life and those of his friends. Further, he will erect a barrier of electric wires to protect his mountaintop fortress, and similarly will employ his scientific genius to create other weapons to be deployed should the collectivists make war on him. He knows that in any conflict between mind and brute force, the mind will triumph.

Finally, he is confident about the outcome of any clash between himself and the collectivists due to his awareness of the undying human spirit. Speaking of the heroic freedom fighters of the past about whom he has read, he states that their battle is one that can never be lost; that the liberty they died to save can never perish. The human mind and soul will eternally hunger for freedom; this aspiration can never be killed by any dictator or collectivist state. Humans suffering under the yoke of tyranny will, when liberty is offered to them, seize the opportunity to live as free persons. Prometheus now understands that the human mind requires freedom—successful life on earth requires it—and therefore the soul yearns for it. The human desire for freedom cannot be squelched, and Prometheus's battle cannot be lost.

Glossary

Prometheus legendary titan of Greek mythology who stole fire from the gods and brought it to earth. He was punished by Zeus, who chained him to a rock and had a vulture eat out his liver daily. But thereafter humans had fire to keep warm and to light the darkest night.

Gaea goddess of Greek mythology who gave birth to the earth and to the titans.

City of the Damned city in which Prometheus and Gaea formerly resided, and from which they fled.

Ego the self. That aspect of an individual that thinks, forms values, and makes judgments. Here it refers to the need that individuals have to be liberated of the stifling restraints of collectivism, free to use their own minds and glory in their own individual uniqueness.

CHARACTER ANALYSES

The following critical analyses delve into the physical, emotional, and psychological traits of the literary work's major characters so that you might better understand what motivates these characters. The writer of this study guide provides this scholarship as an educational tool by which you may compare your own interpretations of the characters. Before reading the character analyses that follow, consider first writing your own short essays on the characters as an exercise by which you can test your understanding of the original literary work. Then, compare your essays to those that follow, noting discrepancies between the two. If your essays appear lacking, that might indicate that you need to re-read the original literary work or re-familiarize yourself with the major characters.

Equality 7-2521 (Prometheus)

Equality 7-2521 is a man who holds on to his own mind in a collectivist society that demands blind obedience to the group. The single most important factor in understanding his character is his independence. Despite powerful pressure from the state to conform, he will not betray the values that are important to him. Scientific research is what gives meaning and joy to his life, and he will not abandon it though he knows the severity of the punishment that awaits him if he is caught. Similarly, he dares to love the Golden One though it is forbidden. Finally, he refuses to surrender the electric light to the authorities when he realizes that they will destroy it. He accepts ostracism, banishment, and damnation from his fellow citizens rather than surrender to them his light and his mind.

His independence of thinking and of spirit is what explains his actions from the earliest days of his childhood. Even in his youth, he knew it was the "science of things" that fascinated him. Though it is forbidden to prefer one field to another, he loves science far more than any other field. Though youths are not permitted to desire a profession of their own choosing, he yearns to be sent to the Home of the Scholars where he can pursue the research he loves. In his first significant act of the present-time story, he discovers an abandoned subway tunnel and ventures into it. Though he knows that the Councils do not permit it, and though he further realizes that the tunnel is a remnant of the Unmentionable Times—to be scrupulously shunned—he explores it immediately and afterward tells his friend it belongs to him. Then he proceeds to steal materials and manuscripts, employing the tunnel for a private laboratory in which to conduct experiments. It is necessary to realize that all of these actions are not merely prohibited, they are *unthinkable* in this society. Such thoughts do not occur to men in this culture. For example, when Equality 7-2521 informs International 4-8818 that they will not report their discovery of the tunnel, his friend is flabbergasted. International 4-8818, though himself an exceptionally independent man, raises his hands to his ears, "for never had they heard such words as these." The obvious meaning is that such words had never been spoken or even thought.

Clearly, Equality 7-2521 is a genius. Under unspeakably arduous conditions, and in the face of bitter antagonism from the powerful authorities who oppose him, he proceeds to advance the state of humankind's knowledge by an enormous leap. With only his own talent and initiative—with nothing but obstacles contributed by others—

Equality 7-2521 is able to reinvent the electric light in a society that has only recently made the progress from torches to candles. This invention is an extraordinary testimony to his own genius and perseverance.

Equality 7-2521 is a fictitious example of the great thinkers of history who have made revolutionary breakthroughs in spite of the social antagonism they faced. Such individuals as Louis Pasteur, Charles Darwin, Marie Curie, Robert Fulton, the Wright Brothers, and many others were scientists and inventors whose discoveries and innovations overturned previous thinking. Such geniuses were not only confronted by the difficulty of identifying nature's secrets but also by the antagonism of the society whose beliefs they challenged. Great creative thinkers such as Equality 7-2521 are motivated by the love of their work— whether it is biology, medicine, or physics or in such areas of the humanities as literature, music, or philosophy. Their passion keeps them going despite the inherent difficulties of making intellectual breakthroughs and of battling the conservative elements of society that oppose them. Equality 7-2521 will not surrender his creative work no matter the degree or variety of difficulties he encounters.

This persistence is a measure of his integrity. He lives by his convictions regardless of the obstacles that confront him. For a man to possess the virtue of integrity, he must be true in action to the principles and values that he holds. He must practice what he preaches. Equality 7-2521 possesses integrity to an exceptional degree, for he not only lives in accordance with his values through the normal vicissitudes of life, but more tellingly, even when in conflict with a stifling dictatorship that outlaws his creative work and threatens to punish his actions by death. If a man knows that a career of scientific research is right for him and pursues it even though opposed by his family, that is admirable. But if he pursues it in a social context where the state decrees against it—and where individuality has been so expunged that all conceptions of independent thinking are foreign to all—that is extraordinary. Equality 7-2521 is a fictitious example of the kind of heroes responsible for the progress that real society has achieved.

His relationship with the Golden One also displays his integrity. He clearly knows that she stands out from all other women. When she asks him if he would look at her in a crowd of other women, he replies that he would look upon her if she were with all the women of the earth. Though it is forbidden for men to think of women at any period other than the Time of Mating, he thinks of her often. Though it is forbidden for men and women to speak to each other, he initiates a conversation with her. Though the Councils are all-powerful, he decides that he will not permit them to ever take the Golden One to the Palace of Mating. When he must flee the city under threat of death, his inability to see her is his one regret. Again, his commitment in action to his values stands out. He will not yield the things he wants out of life, no matter the struggle it takes to attain them.

Finally, his integrity reaches also to his quest for freedom. No doubt his greatest achievement is his realization—in a society that does everything possible to stifle it—that human beings are individuals, and that they require political freedom to live. His re-discovery of individualism, embodied by his identification of the word "I", is not an isolated incident in his life. It is the outcome of a lifelong commitment, in practice, to the principles of independent functioning. He knows he wants to be a scientist, he wonders about the Unspeakable Word, he performs secret experiments and woos the Golden One though both are strictly forbidden. Throughout his life, he is true to his own mind, never a blind follower of the state. *He lives like an individual long before he discovers the concept of individualism.* Because of his unbreached commitment to his mind, he chooses the path that ultimately leads to his re-discovery of the individual mind. In some unspoken way that he could not articulate, Equality 7-2521 knew from childhood that human beings are individuals who must live by their own minds—and this is the way he always lives. Logically, his independent functioning leads to the re-discovery of independence.

Liberty 5-3000 (Gaea)

Liberty 5-3000 (or the Golden One, as so named by Equality) is a perfect match for Equality 7-2521. She, too, has a mind of her own that refuses to blindly follow the authorities. She is more than a beautiful young woman; she is a woman whose inner beauty is externally recognizable. Long before speaking to her, Equality 7-2521 knows the virtues she possesses. He sees that her body is "straight and thin as a blade of iron." Her eyes are dark and hard, devoid of both fear and guilt. Her hair flies wild in the wind, as if defying men to restrain it. She throws seeds to the ground as if scornfully dispensing a gift, and it seems as if the earth is "a beggar under her feet." Equality 7-2521 gleans from her straightness of carriage, her fearless eyes, and her derisive mannerisms that she is proud, with an inner reverence that comes only from an unbroken independence of spirit.

Her spirit is displayed in her actions as well as in her appearance. She too violates the laws and customs of her society to pursue her goals. For example, she observes Equality 7-2521 and thinks of him, though the state forbids a woman to take notice of men except at the Time of Mating. She walks boldly to the hedge bordering the road and looks him in the face. She smiles at him, and they speak to each other with their eyes. She subsequently talks to him as fearlessly as he does to her. She tells him that he is not one of her brothers—as are other men—because she does not wish him to be. Later, she says she has given him a name, as he has to her. She thinks of him in her own mind as The Unconquered. Not only does she admire him for his unbroken spirit, but also in the act of forming these forbidden thoughts, she demonstrates her own unconquered soul. She honors him for the best qualities within herself. In the end, she must choose between acceptance in her society—the only life she has ever known—and rejection, even probable death, with Equality 7-2521, and she makes an unhesitating choice. Social approval means nothing to her; her own personal values mean everything. She tells him in the forest, "We wish to be damned with you, rather than blessed with all our brothers." She exhorts him not to send her back to the city.

The Golden One's character, like that of Equality 7-2521, illustrates an important principle regarding the author's theory of human nature: independent persons form values of their own. The Golden One does not passively accept the beliefs of society. For example, she is not an egalitarian who believes there are no distinctions to be made among persons and that each is the equal of all. She does not love her brothers and sisters equally. Like her lover, she commits the "sin" of preference—and does so proudly. She recognizes that distinct persons are not equal in an absolute sense, and she loves Equality 7-2521 because his genius and proud independence cause him to stand out from the crowd. Because she thinks for herself, she *values* for herself, she decides by her own thinking what she will consider important or of significant worth. She chooses Equality 7-2521 for her own reasons and in defiance of social regulations. She chooses to pursue him into the forest for those same reasons, despite knowing that such a decision represents a literal point of no return: she will not be re-admitted into society and believes there is a good chance she will die in the forest. An independent thinker is a valuer, not a follower.

Her independence of evaluation is responsible for the vitality of her emotional life in contrast to the desiccated existences of her peers. Because other members of society mindlessly conform, they have no passions of their own. They value nothing in the way that Equality 7-2521 values scientific research and the Golden One, or in the way that she values him. They love nothing so much that they are willing to creep around in a dark tunnel to perform experiments—or flee alone into a dangerous forest to seek the person they desire. Nothing means that much to the other members of society because they have surrendered their minds to the state. Persons who do not think for themselves cannot value for themselves, and they end up with stunted emotional lives. The other members of this society are emotionless drones because their lives are empty. They have chosen to blindly follow the state, to seek no personal values, and consequently, to experience no great passion. The Golden One repudiates such a course of action emphatically. She knows what she wants and goes after it. Society's beliefs are insufficient to shake her confidence in her own judgment, and this is what makes her a heroine.

International 4-8818

International 4-8818 is a friend of Equality 7-2521 because he possesses the same independent spirit as do the hero and heroine. Equality 7-2521 states that, "International 4-8818 and we are friends." Both men recognize this fact and understand that they commit the "great Transgression of Preference." They both know that they are required to befriend all equally, but neither care. They do not speak of it, for it is dangerous to express such personal thoughts, but their relationship is understood by both. "We know when we look into each other's eyes." Because of International 4-8818's autonomous soul, he is a free spirited youth who possesses laughter in his eyes. Equality 7-2521 states that he cannot look upon his friend and refrain from smiling. International 4-8818 was not liked for his perpetual joy in the Home of Students, for in this oppressive society it is not permitted to smile without reason. He was disliked for a deeper reason, as well. He drew pictures on the walls with pieces of charcoal—happy pictures that made men laugh. But the authorities forbid drawing to all but those sent to the Home of the Artists, so International 4-8818 is punished for his transgressions. Because the authorities recognize his independent spirit, they are scared of him. As with Equality 7-2521, they seek to discourage International 4-8818's autonomy of spirit, so they send him to the Home of the Street Sweepers. Here, he will not to be allowed to draw, as Equality 7-2521 is not allowed to perform scientific experiments. By taking from these heroic men the values they love, the state seeks to eventually break their spirits.

International 4-8818's true nature is revealed in his most important action of the story—his role in the discovery of the abandoned subway tunnel. When Equality 7-2521 decides to explore the tunnel, which is clearly a remnant of the Unmentionable Times, International 4-8818 does not stop him. More telling is his friend's response when Equality 7-2521 states that the tunnel belongs to him and is not to be reported to the authorities. At first, International 4-8818 covers his ears with his hands, for never in his life has he heard thoughts such as these expressed. But then Equality 7-2521 reminds him that if they report his solo exploration of the tunnel, the authorities will lash him to death before International 4-8818's eyes. Equality 7-2521 asks International 4-8818 whether he would be party to this. International 4-8818 "stood straight of a sudden and they answered, 'Rather would we die.'" He refuses to turn Equality 7-2521 in, though he knows that to cover up the truth is a major sin in this society. He reminds Equality 7-2521 that the will of their brothers is holy and above all other things. But if Equality 7-2521 wishes it this way, he says, then so be it. "Rather shall we be evil with you than good with all our brothers." He stays true to his friendship with Equality 7-2521 through all the events of the story. He never breathes a word to anyone through the years of Equality 7-2521's secret research when his friend slips away from the City Theatre for hours every night. International 4-8818, like Equality 7-2521 and the Golden One, possesses a mind and values of his own, and he refuses to betray them.

For this reason, Equality 7-2521 plans to steal back into the city and rescue International 4-8818. His good friend has managed to develop his own mind, and there is no place for him in the stifling collectivist society in which he is trapped. But in the free society that Equality 7-2521 seeks to find in the mountains, men will be able to pursue their dreams. There, International 4-8818 will be free to draw as he likes and to think for himself. He has abundantly earned the chance to live as a free man, and Equality 7-2521 intends to provide it for him. International 4-8818 will be the first to defect from the global dictatorship and find freedom in the new society. He will escape to liberty just as many have fled from such Communist states as Cuba, North Korea, Vietnam, China, and various nations of Eastern Europe. International 4-8818 will not be the last to flee collectivism, for as news spreads that human beings again have a chance for freedom, the most independent among them will re-initiate the quest that had flourished centuries earlier: They will defect in droves and seek political asylum in the free country.

The Saint of the Pyre

Although this character appears only in a flashback and does not figure in the present-time action, he is an important person in the story. He is a young man whom Equality 7-2521, in his youth, witnesses being burned at the stake. The young man had re-discovered and dared to state the Unspeakable Word. The authorities had ripped his tongue from his throat, so he could speak no more. The youthful Equality 7-2521 sees that the transgressor is young and tall, with gold hair and eyes as "blue as morning." He walks to his death with a sure step. Among the shrieking masses at the public execution, his is the calmest and happiest face. As the authorities wind chains around his body, lashing him to the stake, Equality 7-2521 notices that a thread of blood runs from his mouth, but that his lips are curled in a smile. The young Equality 7-2521 experiences a thought then that, given his indoctrination, he regards as traitorous. He had been taught of the Saints of Labor, the Saints of the Councils, and the Saints of the Great Rebirth. But up until that time, he had seen neither a Saint nor a picture of one. The idea comes to him that this courageous youth, who faces death calmly, bears the likeness of a Saint—that his noble bearing is what one would properly expect of a moral paragon.

As the flames rise to engulf him, a strange thing happens. The Saint's eyes rove the crowd and stop on the youthful Equality 7-2521, singling him out for attention. The Saint stares at him with neither pain nor fear, but with a seemingly holy joy and with pride. It seems to the young Equality 7-2521 that the Saint is trying to communicate with him, seeking to impart some precious knowledge. The Saint attempts to teach Equality 7-2521 the sound and the meaning of the Unspeakable Word—but the flames sweep over his body, leaving him no chance. It leaves Equality 7-2521 with an agonizing question regarding the Unspeakable Word, and a determination to discover its meaning, even if, as the Saint, he must burn at the pyre for it.

The Saint's character embodies a significant element of foreshadowing. The Saint of the Pyre recognizes in Equality 7-2521's height, posture, and fearless gaze the same independence of spirit that he possesses and singles him out as the next brave soul who will re-discover the word embodying the meaning of individualism. This scene presents a symbolic changing of the guard, a passing of the torch from a dying hero to the young man who, in the future, will carry the battle to its successful conclusion.

CRITICAL ESSAYS

On the pages that follow, the writer of this study guide provides critical scholarship on various aspects of Ayn Rand's *Anthem*. These interpretive essays are intended solely to enhance your understanding of the original literary work; they are supplemental materials and are not to replace your reading of *Anthem*. When you're finished reading *Anthem*, and prior to your reading this study guide's critical essays, consider making a bulleted list of what you think are the most important themes and symbols. Write a short paragraph under each bullet explaining *why* you think that theme or symbol is important; include at least one short quote from the original literary work that supports your contention. Then, test your list and reasons against those found in the following essays. Do you include themes and symbols that the study guide author doesn't? If so, this self test might indicate that you are well on your way to understanding original literary work. But if not, perhaps you will need to re-read *Anthem*.

The Meaning and Importance of "I"

One of the most striking features of *Anthem* is its use of language, especially the absence of the word "I." Characters refer to themselves using the first person plural "we" and not the first person singular "I." This use of language is often confusing, but must be understood if the book's meaning is to be clear. The use of the plural rather than the singular self-reference, goes to the heart of the book's meaning.

The collectivist society in which Equality 7-2521 lives is similar to the Nazi and Communist states of the twentieth century. The rulers of this society do not permit any individual to think freely; all must subordinate themselves to the state. "Collectivism," Ayn Rand notes, "means the subjugation of the individual to the group—whether to a race, class or state does not matter." Under such conditions, a person is not regarded as an autonomous individual with a life of his or her own, but as a fragment of a group whose sole purpose is to serve its needs.

The rulers of Equality 7-2521's society seek to discourage even the realization of individuality; they attempt to inculcate an "ant colony" mentality in which human beings emulate the self-sacrificial existence of insects serving the overall good of the whole. The authorities wish to expunge from human nature all thoughts of individuality and, as a consequence, all elements of a personal life in action. No one has a personal name; instead each is tagged with generalized concepts of collectivism such as Equality, International, Solidarity, and so on. This attempt to extirpate all elements of individuality similarly explains why each person has a number attached to this collectivist label. Because the state considers individuality unreal, no person is unique or outstanding, human beings are interchangeable parts of a greater whole.

As a further means toward the obliteration of individuality, the state has forbidden friendship and romantic love. These elements of individuality are considered examples of the Transgression of Preference, the act of singling one person out of the mass of humankind for purposes of establishing a close relationship.

But the state's main weapon against individualism is the crude but effective form of thought control that it practices. The state has forbidden humans from speaking or even thinking of the word "I." Society has mandated, under punishment of death, that all first-person references are with the plural "we," even when the reference is to a single person. Over a period of centuries, the rulers have managed to extirpate all knowledge of the word "I" from the language. All that remains is a vague memory that there is such a thing as an Unspeakable Word—but no one has an inkling that it is the word "I."

Despite the primitive backwardness of this collectivist society, the power of its suppressive methods must be recognized. The dictators have succeeded in subjugating the populace in ways that go beyond the stifling policies of such murderous tyrants as Hitler, Stalin, Mao Zedong, and Pol Pot. These real-life collectivist rulers forced millions of human beings to surrender their individuality *in practice.* The dictatorial regimes of Nazi Germany, Soviet Russia, Communist China, and Communist Cambodia forced their citizens, in action, to serve the state. Individuals had no right to their own lives, and their actions were brutally controlled; they were slaves of Nazism or Communism.

But even these bloody dictatorships were not able to so alter the very terms in which humans think as to eradicate the *vocabulary of individuality.* The fictitious state of the novel has succeeded in expunging all concepts of independent personhood, wiping out human beings' means to even think as individuals. This act is the most thorough form of thought control ever devised. The deluded citizens have only one self-concept available to them—splintered fragments of the group. Everyone thinks of themselves as merely nameless, faceless, individuality-less chunks of an amorphous mass.

The state succeeds in eliminating all thoughts of independent existence for many years, perhaps centuries. The Saint of the Pyre is the only man who re-discovers the existence and meaning of the word "I"—and he is condemned to death. The other members of society do not even wonder about what is missing from their lives. Equality 7-2521, however, says that the sight of the Saint being burned has stayed with him, "it haunts us and follows us, and it gives us no rest." More than the injustice of a hero tortured to death haunts Equality 7-2521; it is a desire to know the Unspeakable Word at all costs. "What—even if we have to burn for it—is the Unspeakable Word?"

He is alone with these tormenting thoughts until the Golden One joins him on the quest to discover this lost word. Attempting to express her feelings, she realizes the inadequacy of the vocabulary available to her. "No . . . We are one . . . alone . . . and only . . . and we love you who are one . . . alone . . . and only." Two threads intertwine here. They know of the Unspeakable Word. They also recognize that they are unable to properly express themselves in the first person. In short order, they come to realize that the two issues are the same.

Despite the suppressive methods of the Councils, some members of this society retain individuality. Equality 7-2521 wonders ceaselessly about the lost word. He maintains the secret of the tunnel and uses it for his forbidden research. He decides that the Golden One is not to be touched by the Councils' policies of state-controlled breeding. He is a man who stands tall. But he does not have to stand alone. Others in this society have not surrendered their minds to the rulers.

International 4-8818, like Equality 7-2521, commits the Transgression of Preference; he selects Equality 7-2521 as his friend from the mass of humanity. Upon hearing Equality 7-2521's astounding words that they will not report the tunnel, International 4-8818 covers his ears, for never has he heard such words. But he chooses to risk death with his friend rather than obey the councils. "Rather shall we be evil with you than be good with all our brothers." He covers for Equality 7-2521 during the years in which he conducts his illicit research and never betrays him.

Liberty 5-3000, the Golden One, similarly refuses to surrender her independence to the state. She, too, defies the decrees of the councils to achieve her ends. She notices Equality 7-2521, though she is supposed to take no heed of men. She names him in her mind The Unconquered. She speaks to him against all the rules. She abandons the city and the only life she has ever known, venturing alone into the Uncharted Forest to find him. In the end, it is she who, unaided, comes closest to re-discovering the Unspeakable Word when, in the forest, she gropes for the words with which to accurately express her feelings. She is an individualist like Equality 7-2521 and International 4-8818.

Despite the policies of the councils, a few members of this society retain their independence while the majority surrender their souls to the state. Why is it that a few resist while the majority acquiesces? What sets apart from the crowd of followers such heroic individualists as Equality 7-2521, International 4-8818, and the Golden One?

The answer the author gives is that some exceptional individuals refuse to give up their minds to authority. Equality 7-2521 and his allies understand, even without the words, that human beings are by nature *rational animals* and that thinking is an individualistic activity. "I think" is the essence of their being.

The Role of Free Will in *Anthem*

Ayn Rand depicts characters that make important choices; her characters select from alternatives available to them—significant and sometimes life-and-death issues. Equality 7-2521 is the most obvious example, but not the only character in the book to make such choices. He chooses to wonder about the Unspeakable Word when he could (and, according to this society, should) decide not to. He chooses to conceal both the existence of the tunnel and his experiments, refusing to bow to the Councils' will. He chooses not to tell his captors where he has been though they torture him. He selects International 4-8818 and the Golden One for his intimates from all members of society. He chooses to flee into the wilderness rather than turn his light and his life over to the Councils. In his undaunted willingness to take control of his life, he is the most compelling example of this capacity to choose.

The negative characters make choices as well. The most obvious example is the one made by the World Council of Scholars when Equality 7-2521 presents the electric light. After recovering from their fear, they recognize the value the light possesses. They know the invention will put out of business the newly developed candle industry and will upset the plans of the World Councils, who will now have to incorporate the new invention into society. It is not that the Scholars do not see the light's value. The question is whether they want to take advantage of its value. The alternatives before them are starkly clear: electricity, technological progress, and independent thought; or candles, technological backwardness, and thought control. They make their choice. They select more than candles over electric light; they choose suppression and dictatorship over independence and political freedom. They choose primitive stagnation over progress. They choose squalor and misery over prosperity. They choose the same path of conformity they have followed all their lives rather than an uncharted course of independent thinking. The Scholars have the power to make important choices. Unfortunately, they choose based on their lust for power.

Equality 7-2521's friends also have free will. International 4-8818 makes an understated but important choice in the story. He is faced with a difficult decision when Equality 7-2521 states that they will not report the existence of the tunnel. If he decides not to report it, he is going against everything he has been taught, every law decreed by the Councils and, consequently, is risking his life. If, on the other hand, he chooses to inform the Councils, he not only violates the trust of his good friend but also likely condemns his friend to a death sentence.

International 4-8818 makes the extraordinary decision to repudiate everything he has learned to stand by Equality 7-2521. If he makes a different choice, Equality 7-2521 is lashed to death before he ever begins his research, he does not invent the electric light, and he does not discover the meaning of the word "I." International 4-8818's choice to support Equality 7-2521 is vital to the outcome of this conflict.

The Golden One likewise makes a life-altering decision in the face of alternatives. When she hears that Equality 7-2521 has fled into the Uncharted Forest, she is confronted by a difficult dilemma. If she chooses to pursue Equality 7-2521, she faces excommunication from the only society she has known and probable (from her perspective) death in the untamed wilderness. But if she selects the physical and psychological safety of the culture in which she was raised, then she loses the man she loves. The Golden One's choice is as bold as International 4-8818's. She chooses to risk all, including her life, to find Equality 7-2521. In her choice, too, the stakes are high. If she selects the safety of conformity, then Equality 7-2521 is alone, and his attempt to initiate a new society is undercut by his lack of a wife.

Even the society of drones who blindly follow the edicts of the Councils are shown to do so voluntarily. These people are not brainwashed by means of drugs or physical torture; they are not beaten into submission. Rather, they simply conform. They go along with what they are taught. *They do not question the councils, even in their own minds.* They are not like Equality 7-2521 or the Golden One. They show no independence of spirit. It is true that no open dissent is tolerated by the rulers—and punishment for disobedience is swift and, in some cases, terminal. But none of the followers shows any indication that, like Equality 7-2521, they have nurtured—in private and quietly—a mind of their own. The entire populace of the city stood in the public square and witnessed the execution of the Saint of the Pyre. But so far as we know, none of the others is haunted by the memory nor seeks the meaning of the Unspeakable Word. Certainly, nobody but Equality 7-2521 defies the Council's commands to pursue personal values. All that the citizens have been taught is that the wisdom of the Councils is complete—so they accept it and obey.

The members of this society, including the adults, are like obedient children who unquestioningly accept what their parents tell them. Equality 7-2521, the Golden One, and International 4-8818 question the Councils in their own minds; the others accept what they are told. In the face of the alternative between independent thinking and blind compliance, different individuals make different choices.

It would be mistaken to morally condemn the masses for their unwillingness to keep alive their own minds and spirits. They are not evil but are cowed by the authoritarianism of the rulers. The Councils that mandate blind obedience are evil. Rather, the intriguing question raised by the heroic characters is how they manage to keep alive their own minds in the face of such oppressive pressure to conform. Ayn Rand's purpose is not to criticize the crowd, but to glorify the rare individuals who know, against all teaching and social pressure, that their minds are sacred and not to be surrendered to authority.

Such individuals exist in real life, as well. Children who are raised by tyrannical parents rebel against the arbitrary dogma forced on them. Closer to the situation of *Anthem* are those brave souls who oppose the governments of Nazi or Communist regimes, men and women who are dissidents or even members of an armed resistance. Countries such as Russia, China, and various East European states were or have been Communist for many decades, with entire generations born, raised, and educated under collectivism. Most of the populace of these countries, as depicted in *Anthem*, accepted and followed the teachings of their leaders. But some chose to be dissidents, risking their lives by speaking out against the regime, seeking greater freedom, and in many cases going to prison or concentration camps for their convictions. Many were executed for their outspoken activities. The extraordinary heroism displayed by Equality 7-2521, International 4-8818, and the Golden One lacks neither historical precedent nor current example.

But such courage remains extraordinary. No deeper factors necessitate Equality 7-2521's independence. That nothing necessitates his use of the mind is what makes it a choice. However, the question can be asked: What makes it possible? With what faculty or power does he resist the oppressive dogma of his society? The author's answer is that *the nature of the individual is to be a thinker*. Just as a bird's nature is to fly, a lion's is to hunt, and a cow's is to give milk, so a human's is to think. Birds have wings, lions have claws, and so on. Humans have brains, and successful living on earth requires them to use them. An oppressive family or society, in requiring blind conformity, fights a war against human nature, which is to be a thinking being.

The dictators may succeed in cowing large elements of the populace, convincing them to meekly grovel—but they will never succeed in changing human nature. Their mandates are powerless to alter the earth's orbit around the sun or a plant's necessity to conduct photosynthesis or a bird's need to fly. Similarly, their commands cannot change the fact that a human is a thinking being. Therefore, the possibility of thinkers arising to question those who wish to subjugate others cannot be extirpated.

Dictators fight an endless battle against human nature, for every infant born in every year is a potential threat; they cannot afford to stunt the intellectual development of merely most. *The dictators must get them all.* For even one like Equality 7-2521—even one Copernicus or Galileo or Darwin or Thomas Jefferson—is a grave danger to their power. The rulers must be ceaselessly, zealously on guard, regarding the brain of every baby as a potential death threat. The tyrants, in battling human nature, face a hopeless task and are doomed to lose. In every birth is the possibility of an extraordinary individual such as Equality 7-2521, one who chooses human nature rather than the arbitrary dogma of a dictator. These are the heroes responsible for humanity's rise from prehistoric savagery to modern civilization.

There have been dogmatists and dictators from the dawn of history—religious, political, even familial—who in their quest for power have sought to stifle the human mind. Again and again, they have carved out their fiefdoms and declared the human duty to obey; empires have lasted for generations, even centuries. But in the end, thinkers such as Equality 7-2521 arise, who know from childhood that their allegiance is to their mind, not their ruler, and who set forth new thoughts. The age old battle has gone by many names—in *Anthem*, it is the individual versus the collective—but the primordial antagonists, though taking varying forms, remain the same: those who champion the mind and those who stifle it. This is the fundamental choice confronted by human beings. In *Anthem*, those on each side are clear.

The Regression of a Future Collectivist Society into a Second Dark Age

The question must be asked: Why does the author depict this totalitarian state of the future as a primitive, technologically backward society? The answer lies in Ayn Rand's theory regarding the cause of production and wealth. Examples of her theory abound in the novel. It is important to note that the hero is an inventor. He has been enthralled by the phenomena of nature since childhood. He loves the "science of things." He desires above all to be a scholar, a scientific researcher. He is so committed to this dream that he faces hardship and endures every difficulty to accomplish it. He is a genius—a

Thomas Edison of the future—who in the teeth of every form of opposition, re-invents the electric light. The essential point is that Equality 7-2521 is a man of the mind. He is a thinker, a man of reason. An invention such as the electric light is a product of the mind.

Rand argues that all aspects of progress—scientific research, medical advances, inventions, technological improvements, industrial production—are achievements of the mind. Such accomplishments are not brought about by faith in the supernatural or, primarily, by manual labor, but by the rational mind. Historically, individuals such as Equality 7-2521—thinkers—have been responsible for humankind's greatest advances. Men like Copernicus and Galileo, who established that the sun is the center of the solar system, Charles Darwin, who proved that human life evolved from simpler life forms, the Wright Brothers, who pioneered man's ability to fly, and many more are real-life examples of individuals such as Equality 7-2521. These are men whose minds have discovered vital new truths that significantly improved human life on earth. The overall principle is that human well-being depends on the reasoning mind.

The question Ayn Rand raises in *Anthem* is this: Is some social condition necessary for the creative mind to function properly? Can the thinkers perform their inventive work under any type of political system? Or is rational productivity possible only under certain political conditions? The answer she resoundingly provides is that the independent mind needs freedom.

Again, the details are in the story. Equality 7-2521 discovers a new force of nature. He does not yet realize that it is electricity; he calls it the "power of the sky" because he knows that it is the same force that is responsible for lightning. His identification of this power, and his ability to harness it to create the light, require his unswerving dedication to the laws of nature and the facts of reality. Society's beliefs are irrelevant to this creative process; in this case, they are mistaken. Equality 7-2521, if he is to succeed in his endeavor, must allow himself to be ruled exclusively by the scientific facts of the case. *Nature, not society, sets the terms in all such research and scientific investigations.* The independent mind commits itself to truth, facts, and the laws of nature. If the beliefs and/or laws of society contradict the scientific facts, then the independent thinker dismisses such beliefs as mistaken, which is exactly the case with Equality 7-2521.

The Scholars, as the leading spokespersons for society, regard the electric light as evil. But Equality 7-2521 has come to understand some truths regarding the nature of electricity and knows, from his research and experimentation, that this force can be harnessed to light cities and homes. Part of his proof is the glass box that he shows the Scholars, the light that glows under his control. The beliefs of his brothers are erroneous. The light is not evil; nor is it dangerous in the hands of a man knowledgeable regarding its power. Equality 7-2521 is a man whose mind is committed to the facts. He is not swayed by the irrational beliefs of his brothers. When society denounces Equality 7-2521's thinking and opposes the electric light, he does not bow to their commands. He is committed to truth and to the scientific facts, not to the beliefs of others. His is the nature of an independent thinker.

But the rulers of this society have no interest in scientific research or truth. They are interested exclusively in power. In order to maintain their grip over society, they have to control the thinking of their citizens. They cannot allow the mind to function freely. The acquisition and retention of dictatorial power requires the suppression of free thought. Therefore, real-life dictators—whether Fascist, National Socialist, or Communist—always ban freedom of speech, that is, freedom of thought and expression. They know that independent thinkers will disagree with their suppressive policies and, by speaking out, rile the masses against them. Dictators recognize that their most implacable foe is the reasoning mind; for thinkers are concerned solely with truth, not with the arbitrary commands of power-hungry rulers.

A dictator's suppression of the mind necessarily extends to scientific research, as well. Equality 7-2521 is consigned to the Home of the Street Sweepers and denied admission to the ranks of the Scholars because the authorities recognize his brilliant mind and independent spirit and relegate him to the task of unskilled manual labor. They will not encourage the development of his thinking—even if restricted to scientific questions—because they recognize that it is impossible to limit such a mind to science. The dictators are not themselves brilliant men, but they sense in some instinctual way that the mind is their enemy—specifically, that *the mind capable of inventing the electric light or formulating the theory of evolution is just as capable of questioning the moral legitimacy of the dictator's regime.*

Great minds are not necessarily limited to technical questions and concerns; as individual members of the human race, they are often concerned with matters of both personal morality and political philosophy. If they ask such questions and speak out, they are a threat to rouse the people. The common expression, "The pen is mightier than the sword," is true, because the pen is an instrument of the mind. The deeper truth is, "The mind is mightier than the sword," that is, the mind is mightier than brute force. Ayn Rand's point in *Anthem* is that dictators necessarily stifle the mind. In order to maintain their power, they must do so. This is why Equality 7-2521 is refused admittance to the Home of the Scholars and why, later, he is imprisoned, his light threatened, and his life endangered. A great scientist has no chance to flourish in a totalitarian state. In real life, for example, the brilliant physicist, Andrei Sakharov, was persecuted and imprisoned in the Soviet Union for his outspoken moral condemnation of the Soviet invasion of Afghanistan in 1979.

If the entire world is a global dictatorship as in *Anthem*, if freedom exists nowhere on earth, then the mind can seek no haven, no example such as the United States to which one can emigrate in order to gain an independent life. In such a case, the author shows, the mind will be stifled everywhere. There will be no creative thinking or innovation, no scientific research, no technological progress or industrial advance. In a worldwide dictatorship, human society will not move forward.

But the author shows that the implications are even worse. It is not merely the case that humanity will not progress, but that it will regress into a second Dark Age. Society will lose the great accomplishments of the past. If common individuals are to learn from great minds—as they do—they, too, must engage in rational thinking. The successful student, as well as the teacher, must be a thinker. It takes rational thought to learn to operate computers, to service and rebuild airplanes, to perform surgical techniques, to administer plants supplying electrical power, and so on. One does not fly or repair an airplane by rote memorization; one must *understand* the process.

Those who learn from great inventors and discoverers of knowledge are also individuals of the mind. A society that suppresses the mind, that ruthlessly punishes its most independent thinkers, will soon degenerate into a state of primitive barbarism. When the mind is stifled, a society cannot hold onto the technological achievements of the past. An individual, as well as a society, must prove worthy of the achievements inherited from great thinkers of the past. Innovations are the product of freedom and thinking. If humans are no longer free to think, they will lose the creations of the free mind. To see that Ayn Rand depicts an accurate picture in *Anthem*, one can look at the historical Dark Age.

The achievements of the Classical world were many. Plato and Aristotle were extraordinary philosophers, and their schools—the Academy and the Lyceum—flourished for centuries. The dramatists Aeschylus, Sophocles, Euripides, and Aristophanes wrote their brilliant plays in Athens, and the poets Virgil, Horace, and Catullus their great works in Rome. The ancients made advances in medicine, in physics, in mathematics, and in astronomy. Athens was the world's first democratic political system, and its standard of living and life expectancy were both relatively high. Both Greece and Rome, though marred by endless wars and political violence, were essentially civilized societies. Because these societies emphasized reason, they provided freedom, education, and a good life for many citizens.

This all ended in the Dark Age that existed between the fall of Rome and the beginning of the Renaissance. The invading barbarians were men of brute force, not advocates of the mind. They sacked the centers of civilization and, in some cases, burned them to the ground. The barbarians were eventually converted to Christianity, but religion emphasizes faith, not reason. During the period in which the Catholic Church held cultural and political power in Europe, unquestioning obedience to religious dogma was required, and freethinkers were often burned at the stake. Independent thinking was stifled, scientific advance was nonexistent, and illiteracy was rampant. Europeans of this age fell far below the knowledge level, standard of living, and life expectancy that had been attained centuries earlier. They lost the advances that the Classical period had reached. *Because the culture stifled the mind, it lost the rational achievements reached by freer men of the past.* In this regard, the Dark Age of the historical past is an accurate model to the one of the fictional future portrayed in *Anthem.*

Where the primitive society depicted in the story compares closely with the European Dark Age of the medieval period, it contrasts with the collectivist dictatorship presented by George Orwell in his novel, *1984.* Both Rand and Orwell show the unrelieved evil of a collectivist society—the thought control, the necessity to surrender one's mind and life to the state, and the utter lack of individuality and freedom. But despite the two authors' agreement regarding the stifling evil of totalitarianism, an important difference exists between them. Orwell depicts a future collectivist dictatorship as a society that has made great scientific and technological progress. The state employs an ultra-sophisticated technology to engage in mind reading and thought control.

Orwell's theme that a global dictatorship can make scientific advances (or even retain the accomplishments created by freer societies of the past) contrasts sharply with Rand's depiction of collectivism's regression to ignorant savagery. Rand believes that Orwell makes the mistake of believing that the mind can continue to function under compulsion. He does not realize that great achievements are the result of independent thinking by humans such as Equality 7-2521, who recognizes only the truths of nature and who conforms neither to society's irrational beliefs nor to the state's arbitrary commands. In the Dark Age, the independent thinkers were burned, leaving the Church authorities with no one but lackeys following blindly the prescribed dogma. Rand argues that the recent collectivist states, such as the modern Nazis and Communists, are more suppressive of independent thinking than the medieval Church ever was. Therefore, thinkers such as Equality 7-2521 have even less chance to flourish. If anything, a global collectivist dictatorship will sink to a *lower* standard of living than even that of the Dark Ages. Orwell's belief that the mind will continue to create progress—even under the most suppressive political conditions—is not borne out by historical fact and is false.

Ayn Rand grew up in the Communist dictatorship of Soviet Russia and stayed in touch with friends and family in her homeland for as long as possible. She saw firsthand, and fled from, the murderously suppressive policies of Stalin. She knew that any who dared think for themselves, any who criticized the regime, were dragged off by the secret police never to be heard from again. The most independent thinkers, the best creative minds, lived in terror, knowing they dare not speak out. With the best minds murdered or stifled, the country was utterly unable to achieve progress or prosperity. Even with massive help from the free societies of the West, the Soviet dictatorship subsisted in miserable squalor until finally collapsing from its own destitution. Rand had predicted such a result decades earlier in *Anthem*. A collectivist world, she shows, in the absence of freedom anywhere on earth, will permit no independent thinking and will inevitably backslide into primitive conditions. When thinkers such as Equality 7-2521 are suppressed on a global scale, there can be neither scientific progress nor industrial production. The backwardness and poverty depicted in the novel are the only possible results.

CliffsNotes Review

Use this CliffsNotes Review to test your understanding of the original text, and reinforce what you've learned in this book. After you work through the review and essay questions, identify the quote section, and the fun and useful practice projects, you're well on your way to understanding a comprehensive and meaningful interpretation of Ayn Rand's *Anthem*.

Q&A

1. Why does International 4-8818 not tell the Councils about Equality 7-2521's exploration of the abandoned tunnel?

   a. He is afraid to be punished for his part in the forbidden activity.

   b. He protects his friend from being lashed to death.

   c. It isn't important enough.

   d. He forgot.

2. Why does the Golden One pursue Equality 7-2521 into the Uncharted Forest?

   a. She is willing to risk her life to be with the man she loves.

   b. She is an independent woman who goes by her own judgment.

   c. Life in such a slave society is intolerable.

   d. All of the above.

3. After inventing the electric light, why does Equality 7-2521 want to know about his appearance?

   a. He has become vain.

   b. Now he can see himself.

   c. He has increased pride in himself.

   d. He wonders what the Golden One will think.

4. Why is the Saint of the Pyre burned at the stake?

   a. He discovered and spoke the forbidden word.

   b. He befriended Equality 7-2521.

   c. He tried to escape from the collectivist dictatorship.

   d. He defied the Council of Vocations by refusing to sweep streets.

5. Where does Equality 7-2521 perform his scientific research?

   a. In an abandoned tunnel of the Unmentionable Times.

   b. In the cellar of the Home of Scholars.

   c. In an old barn by the river.

   d. In the Uncharted Forest.

6. In what form is the story of *Anthem* written?

   a. As Equality 7-2521's diary.

   b. As a series of newspaper accounts.

   c. As a biography written by the Golden One after Equality 7-2521's death.

   d. As a report to the Councils.

   Answers: (1) b. (2) d. (3) c. (4) a. (5) a. (6) a.

Fill in the Blank

1. The theme of *Anthem* is _____.

2. The story takes place in _____ .

3. The word "I" is forbidden as _____ .

4. Equality 7-2521 loves the Golden One because _____ .

5. The Scholars recommend Equality 7-2521 be executed because _____
_____ .

6. In the Uncharted Forest, Equality 7-2521 finds _____ .

   Answers: (1) the individual versus the collective. (2) a collectivist dictatorship of the future. (3) a means of extirpating individualism. (4) of her independent spirit. (5) he thought and acted alone. (6) a home from the Unmentionable Times.

Identify the Quote: Find Each Quote in *Anthem*

1. "We are one . . . alone . . . and only . . . and we love you who are one . . . alone . . . and only."

2. "I Am. I Think. I Will."

3. "What is not thought by all men cannot be true."

4. "This place is ours. This place belongs to us, and to no other men on earth. And, if ever we surrender it, we shall surrender our life with it also."

5. "No single man can possess greater wisdom than the many Scholars who are elected by all men for their wisdom. Yet we can. We do."

6. "We are nothing. Mankind is all. By the grace of our brothers are we allowed our lives. We exist through, by and for our brothers who are the State. Amen."

Answers: (1) The Golden One speaking to Equality 7-2521 after their escape from the city. She comes close to grasping the concept of "I" in this statement, but the forbidden word still eludes them. (2) Equality 7-2521 after he discovers the Unspeakable Word by means of reading the ancient texts. He now exults in his own individuality and in his liberation not only from the collectivist society but also from its thinking. (3) Collective 0-0009 speaking to Equality 7-2521 after the young inventor demonstrates his electric light to the Scholars. The Scholars recognize that the independence of Equality 7-2521's thought and action is a threat to the collectivist dictatorship. Therefore, they seek to destroy both the inventor and his invention. (4) Equality 7-2521 speaking to International 4-8818 after his discovery and exploration of the abandoned subway tunnel. That Equality 7-2521 could think and act on such forbidden thoughts shows his independence—and makes possible his research. (5) Equality 7-2521 writing in his diary after his discovery of the power of electricity. His words express his germinating realization that the group isn't always right, and that one individual can know better than an entire society. (6) The oath taken nightly by the children in the Home of the Students. It expresses the essence of the collectivism with which they are daily indoctrinated by this society.

Essay Questions

1. Why does the Council of Vocations assign Equality 7-2521 to sweeping the streets?

2. Why do the collectivists prohibit knowledge of the word "I"?

3. What is referred to by the Unmentionable Times? What were conditions like in that period of history?

4. In what way does the love relationship between Equality 7-2521 and the Golden One violate the fundamental beliefs of this society?

5. Why do several of Equality 7-2521's fellow street sweepers cry suddenly and/or scream in the night? What does their unhappiness say about both human nature and conditions in this society?

6. Why do the Scholars condemn the electric light even though they recognize its effectiveness?

Practice Projects

1. Enact in class a scene in which the mature Equality 7-2521, protected by devices powered by electricity, confronts the World Council. What would he say to them? How would they respond?

2. Create a dialogue among students between Equality 7-2521 and other great creative minds of history who have been persecuted, such as Socrates, Galileo, Darwin, and Pasteur. Research some of these accomplished thinkers and, with students in the role of each, discuss with Equality 7-2521 the hardships of thinking innovatively in a society hostile to new ideas.

3. Create a Web site to introduce *Anthem* to other readers. Design pages to explain the novel's theme to your audience and invite other readers to post their thoughts on the book.

4. Hold a debate in class with Equality 7-2521 and the Golden One on one side and the Councils on the other. What points would the Councils make in defense of collectivism? What points would Equality 7-2521 and the Golden One make in defense of individualism?

5. Discuss in class the contemporary relevance of *Anthem's* theme. Are there countries founded on collectivist premises that are similar to those shown in the book? If so, what are conditions like in those countries? Are there countries founded on the individualist premises held by Equality 7-2521 and the Golden One? If so, what are conditions like in those countries? Which type of society would you rather live in, and why?

CliffsNotes Resource Center

The learning doesn't need to stop here. CliffsNotes Resource Center shows you the best of the best—links to the best information in print and online about Ayn Rand and works written by and about her. And don't think that this is all we've prepared for you; we've put all kinds of pertinent information at www.cliffsnotes.com. Look for all the terrific resources at your favorite bookstore or local library and on the Internet. When you're online, make your first stop www.cliffsnotes.com, where you'll find more useful information about *Anthem*.

Books

If you're looking for more information about Ayn Rand and her other works, check out these publications.

Critical Works about Rand

Letters of Ayn Rand, edited by Michael Berliner, provides a collection of Ayn Rand's letters on topics ranging from Objectivism to advice for beginning writers. Includes an introduction by Leonard Peikoff. New York: Plume, 1997.

The Ayn Rand Lexicon: Objectivism from A to Z, edited by Harry Binswanger, offers an alphabetically arranged collection of Rand's writings on her philosophy of Objectivism. New York: New American Library Trade, 1990.

The Journals of Ayn Rand, edited by David Harriman, provides a personal look at Ayn Rand in her own words. Includes Rand's notes for her writing, essays, and thoughts on Hollywood and communism. New York: Plume, 1997.

The Ayn Rand Reader, edited by Gary Hull, contains excerpts from all of Rand's novels. Introduces readers to Rand's writing and philosophy. New York: Plume, 1999.

Objectivism: The Philosophy of Ayn Rand, by Leonard Peikoff, offers a renowned Ayn Rand scholar's explanation of Rand's philosophy. An excellent resource on Rand and Objectivism. New York: Meridian Books, 1993.

The Ominous Parallels, by Leonard Peikoff, explores the causes of Nazism and the parallels between the thought and beliefs in Nazi Germany and the United States. New York: Plume, 1997.

Rand's Major Works of Fiction

Anthem. 1961. New York: Plume, 1999.

Atlas Shrugged. 1957. New York: Signet, 1996.

The Fountainhead. 1943. New York: Signet, 1996.

We the Living. 1936. New York: New American Library, 1996.

The Early Ayn Rand: A Selection from Her Unpublished Fiction. New York: New American Library, 1986.

Rand's Major Works of Nonfiction

Capitalism: The Unknown Ideal. 1967. New York: New American Library, 1984.

For the New Intellectual. 1961. New York: New American Library, 1984.

Introduction to Objectivist Epistemology. Ed. Harry Binswanger and Leonard Peikoff. New York: Meridian Books, 1990.

Philosophy: Who Needs It. 1982. New York: New American Library, 1985.

Return of the Primitive: The Anti-Industrial Revolution. Ed. Peter Schwartz. New York: Meridian Books, 1999.

The Romantic Manifesto. 1971. New York: New American Library, 1975.

Russian Writings on Hollywood. Ed. Michael Berliner. Marina del Ray, California: The Ayn Rand Institute Press, 1999.

The Virtue of Selfishness: A New Concept of Egoism. 1964. New York: New American Library, 1989.

The Voice of Reason: Essays in Objectivist Thought. New York: Meridian Books, 1990.

Internet

Check out these Web resources for more information about Ayn Rand or *Anthem*:

The Ayn Rand Institute, aynrand.org—The Ayn Rand Institute Web site is an outstanding source of information regarding Rand's life, her books, her philosophy, and applications of Objectivism to current events and issues.

Journals of Ayn Rand, www.capitalism.org/journals/index.html—The unofficial Web site for the *Journals of Ayn Rand* offers excerpts from the book as well as comments from scholars and readers.

Next time you're on the Internet, don't forget to drop by www.cliffs notes.com. We created an online Resource Center that you can use today, tomorrow, and beyond.

Films and Audio Recordings

Check out these films and audio recordings for more information on Ayn Rand:

Ayn Rand: A Sense of Life. Dir. Michael Paxton. Perf. Sharon Gless (narrator), Janne Peters, and Peter Sands. AG Media Corporation, Ltd. and Copasetic, Inc., 1997. A documentary film based on Ayn Rand's life.

Love Letters. Dir. William Dieterle. Perf. Jennifer Jones and Joseph Cotton. Paramount Pictures, 1945. A feature film written by Ayn Rand.

You Came Along. Dir. John Farrow. Perf. Robert Cummings and Lizabeth Scott. Paramount Pictures, 1945. A feature film written by Ayn Rand.

You can find these films and recordings for sale on the Internet or for rent at most local libraries and video stores.

Send Us Your Favorite Tips

In your quest for learning, have you ever experienced that sublime moment when you figure out a trick that saves time or trouble? Perhaps you realized that you were taking ten steps to accomplish something that could've taken two. Or, you found a little-known workaround that gets great results. If you've discovered a useful tip that helped you study more effectively and you'd like to share it, the CliffsNotes staff would love to hear from you. Go to our Web site at www.cliffsnotes.com and click the Talk to Us button. If we select your tip, we may publish it as part of CliffsNotes Daily, our exciting, free e-mail newsletter. To find out more or to subscribe to our newsletter, go to www.cliffsnotes.com on the Web.

Index

NUMBERS

AYN RAND ESSAY CONTESTS

$75,000
IN CASH PRIZES

For 9th and 10th Grade High School Students
Annual Essay Contest on Ayn Rand's Novel
ANTHEM

For 11th and 12th Grade High School Students
Annual Essay Contest on Ayn Rand's Novel
THE FOUNTAINHEAD
Top Prize $10,000

For College Business Students
Annual Essay Contest on Ayn Rand's Novelette
ATLAS SHRUGGED

For contest rules, and information on
other college-level contests, visit:

http://www.aynrand.org/contests/

or write to:
Ayn Rand® Essay Contests, P.O. Box 6004, Dept. CN,
Inglewood, CA 90312

CliffsNotes

LITERATURE NOTES

Absalom, Absalom!
The Aeneid
Agamemnon
Alice in Wonderland
All the King's Men
All the Pretty Horses
All Quiet on the Western Front
All's Well & Merry Wives
American Poets of the 20th Century
American Tragedy
Animal Farm
Anna Karenina
Anthem
Antony and Cleopatra
Aristotle's Ethics
As I Lay Dying
The Assistant
As You Like It
Atlas Shrugged
Autobiography of Ben Franklin
Autobiography of Malcolm X
The Awakening
Babbit
Bartleby & Benito Cereno
The Bean Trees
The Bear
The Bell Jar
Beloved
Beowulf
The Bible
Billy Budd & Typee
Black Boy
Black Like Me
Bleak House
Bless Me, Ultima
The Bluest Eye & Sula
Brave New World
The Brothers Karamazov

The Call of the Wild & White Fang
Candide
The Canterbury Tales
Catch-22
Catcher In the Rye
The Chosen
The Color Purple
Comedy of Errors...
Connecticut Yankee
The Contender
The Count of Monte Cristo
Crime and Punishment
The Crucible
Cry, the Beloved Country
Cyrano de Bergerac
Daisy Miller & Turn...Screw
David Copperfield
Death of a Salesman
The Deerslayer
Diary of Anne Frank
Divine Comedy-I. Inferno
Divine Comedy-II. Purgatorio
Divine Comedy-III. Paradiso
Doctor Faustus
Dr. Jekyll and Mr. Hyde
Don Juan
Don Quixote
Dracula
Electra & Medea
Emerson's Essays
Emily Dickinson Poems
Emma
Ethan Frome
The Faerie Queene
Fahrenheit 451
Far from the Madding Crowd
A Farewell to Arms
Farewell to Manzanar
Fathers and Sons
Faulkner's Short Stories

Faust Pt. I & Pt. II
The Federalist
Flowers for Algernon
For Whom the Bell Tolls
The Fountainhead
Frankenstein
The French Lieutenant's Woman
The Giver
Glass Menagerie & Streetcar
Go Down, Moses
The Good Earth
The Grapes of Wrath
Great Expectations
The Great Gatsby
Greek Classics
Gulliver's Travels
Hamlet
The Handmaid's Tale
Hard Times
Heart of Darkness & Secret Sharer
Hemingway's Short Stories
Henry IV Part 1
Henry IV Part 2
Henry V
House Made of Dawn
The House of the Seven Gables
Huckleberry Finn
I Know Why the Caged Bird Sings
Ibsen's Plays I
Ibsen's Plays II
The Idiot
Idylls of the King
The Iliad
Incidents in the Life of a Slave Girl
Inherit the Wind
Invisible Man
Ivanhoe
Jane Eyre
Joseph Andrews
The Joy Luck Club
Jude the Obscure

Julius Caesar
The Jungle
Kafka's Short Stories
Keats & Shelley
The Killer Angels
King Lear
The Kitchen God's Wife
The Last of the Mohicans
Le Morte d'Arthur
Leaves of Grass
Les Miserables
A Lesson Before Dying
Light in August
The Light in the Forest
Lord Jim
Lord of the Flies
The Lord of the Rings
Lost Horizon
Lysistrata & Other Comedies
Macbeth
Madame Bovary
Main Street
The Mayor of Casterbridge
Measure for Measure
The Merchant of Venice
Middlemarch
A Midsummer Night's Dream
The Mill on the Floss
Moby-Dick
Moll Flanders
Mrs. Dalloway
Much Ado About Nothing
My Ántonia
Mythology
Narr. ...Frederick Douglass
Native Son
New Testament
Night
1984
Notes from the Underground

CliffsNotes™

@ cliffsnotes.com

Check Out the All-New CliffsNotes Guides

TECHNOLOGY TOPICS

PERSONAL FINANCE TOPICS

CAREER TOPICS

Made in the USA
Las Vegas, NV
05 December 2022

61224390R00058